WINGS OF CHANCE

WINGS OF CHANCE

By

HAROLD ENSLEY

ISBN: 1-58597-233-9

Library of Congress Control Number: 2003114622

A division of Squire Publishers, Inc.
4500 College Blvd.
Leawood, KS 66211
1/888/888-7696
www.leatherspublishing.com

FOREWORD

This book is a collection of short takes during 50 years of television and radio broadcasting, covering the outdoor scene. The scope on two continents, over a long period of time, makes it difficult to maintain a chronological order.

This is my second book, *Wings of Chance*. I dedicate it to the memory of the late Sam Walton, a special friend and hunting buddy for many years. To the memory of my two favorite bird dogs, Country Squire and Ben, and to dog lovers everywhere, and as I did in my first book, I dedicate this book to all the doctors, nurses, medical technicians and caregivers who kept me alive; to my family and the thousands of people all over the world who have touched my life; to my publisher, Tom Leathers; to David Glass, a special friend; and to Jeanne Boyd, my assistant and caregiver, without whose help I could not have written this book. My sincere thanks, and may God bless you all!

Sincerely,

Harold Ensley

Jeanne, hard at it again!

1

I JUST FINISHED my first book titled "Winds of Chance." This book covered the fishing side of my broadcasting career. I hadn't really planned to do another book covering the hunting side until I was sure that the fishing one was a success. However, I decided that while I was in the mood, to go ahead with it. While I was working on the first book, I told Gloria, my daughter-in-law, that I might sometime write a book on my hunting career. She has been my secretary and office manager, and almost like my right hand for many years. She said, "Why don't you title it *Wings of Chance?*" So *Wings of Chance* it is.

My dad was not a hunter, but like all the ranchers, he owned a shotgun. It was a 12-gauge side-by-side and hammerless. There were not many hammerless guns in the community, and my dad was proud of it. He would occasionally hunt prairie chickens, and once a year the whole community took part in a county-wide rabbit hunt. At that time there were no pheasant or quail in our part of the country. A little creek ran through our ranch, and occasionally Dad would get a chance to shoot a duck. Dad actually killed more young prairie chicken by throwing a hammer or a wrench when he was working the ground, getting the field ready to sow wheat. He worked the fields with horses, and the prairie chickens would just get out of the way of the horses. Dad would stop and throw some object and kill enough for us for a meal. Dad threw left-handed and was deadly with it.

I worked in the field from the time I was 10 years old, driving a team working the ground, but I never killed a prairie chicken the way my dad did. I must have been 12 years old when I got my first gun. It was a Stevens single-shot .22, which I ordered from the Sears catalogue. The county gave a nickel bounty on rabbit ears, 10 cents

Dad and Mom started me doing chores, feeding a calf when I was a little boy.

1

on a crow, and a dollar for a coyote. A bad blizzard swept the prairie, killing hundreds of jackrabbits. I picked up enough for my first rifle. There were no hunter safety classes or rules, and everyone was on his own. You could buy a box of .22 shorts for 40 cents, for 50 cartridges, as I remember. If I were right careful and only shot rabbits sitting at close range, I could get enough rabbits to make a dollar off a box of shells. There were lots of soap weeds on the ranch. The rabbits, in the summertime, would sit in the shade of the soap weeds and be fair game for a barefoot boy. We called them soap weeds, but in reality they were yucca. We trapped in the wintertime, mainly for skunks and muskrats. It wasn't much, but it made us school money. We had to run our trap line in the same clothes we wore to school. It is pretty difficult to handle skunk and not get some of the scent on you. However, we learned that if we got to school before they built a fire in the coal-burning stove, that you couldn't smell the scent. Then when things warmed up, everyone in the room smelled like skunk, even the teacher! Very carefully we managed to get by with it.

When I turned 13, my cousin loaned me his 410 single barrel shotgun. My dad had not yet let me use his 12-gauge, but I thought I had really arrived using the 410. Probably in my age group 90% of the youngsters were given the single shot 410 as a starter. As I look back and analyze the matter, that gun with its hammer might have been, and still might be, the poorest shotgun to start a youngster on. However, in those days it was a matter of money, and there were not many others to choose from. I didn't use it much because of the price of shells. If I remember correctly, I had just turned 16 when they required a hunting license. My dad drove to Dighton, Kansas, the county seat, some 23 miles on a dirt road, to buy my first hunting license. I was in pig heaven! I was now old enough to have a hunting license, and my dad was going to let me use his 12-gauge side-by-side to hunt prairie chickens and ducks. Somehow the firing pin in one barrel was broken, so even though it was a double barrel, you could only operate it as a single barrel gun.

It was about 3 p.m. when we arrived back at the ranch. A small creek ran from the south to the north, into the larger creek that ran through the ranch from west to east. My brother and I had taken shovels and dammed the small creek at the south side of the ranch. It made a small pond about 40 feet wide at the dam, and extended upstream about 50 feet. As we crossed the bridge, we saw five ducks sitting on the pond, two mallard drakes and three teal. They did not fly as we drove on to the ranch house. I asked Dad if I could take the 12-gauge and maybe kill a duck. He kind of smiled as he handed me the gun and a few shells. Here I was, my first time with a 12-gauge shotgun and maybe a chance to kill a duck for the family table. The pond was about a quarter of a mile from our house. The sun was shining, but it was cold. As I made my way, as carefully as possible, I stopped in the sun behind a cut bank and warmed my hands on my body. I was still about 150 yards from the pond, and I knew that I had to sneak the rest of the way to keep from spooking the ducks. There was a shallow ditch, and I crawled the last 20 yards to where I would be right above the pond. I made it, but my hands were so cold that I tried to warm them on my body. I looked up; the ducks had spooked and were in flight about 30 yards high. I stood up quickly and fired at the lead drake. The duck fell like it had run into a stone wall. I was so elated I didn't think about reloading. I ran to pick up the dead duck, and the other ducks flew right back over me about 30 yards high. It would have been a perfect shot at the other drake, but I was so tickled that I had one big fat mallard drake that I didn't worry about the others. It was my first shot with a 12-gauge and I had brought home a duck for the family. As I look back, it may have been one of my most thrilling moments of hunting, and I can see it as though it were yesterday. "Wings of Chance."

I did get to go prairie chicken hunting with Dad's 12-gauge but saw nothing. It was the next year my school chum and I skipped school one day during the season. We shot seven chickens, not our limit, but we were happy and gave the odd one to the school principal.

After graduating from high school, I attended a business college at Hutchinson, Kansas. I had really planned to attend Kansas State to become a geologist, but I didn't have the money. Then, as I remember, they gave scholarships to football players, and possibly basketball. In today's market I likely could have had a chance at one or two in baseball and tennis. I became sidetracked at Hutchinson and at 18 started pitching for a semi-pro team. After a brief stint in baseball, a broken pitching arm sidelined me. I could no longer pitch, but started playing outfield. Then, after a few years of being sidelined by injuries, I gave it up. However, I turned down my last contract offer to play in the Middle Atlantic League. During all that time, I never had much of a chance to hunt. At Joplin, where I began my broadcasting career, some friends took me quail hunting. I didn't even own a gun. They bought an old Model 13 Winchester auto-loading 12-gauge at a garage sale and gave it to me. You loaded it with the barrel. I never saw one like it before or afterward, but it worked! I think it had radar on it, the way it shot.

When I moved to Kansas City, I was so busy with my fishing radio show that I didn't have much time to hunt. However, after Sears bought my radio show to sell shotguns, I was forced to get back into a hunting mode. About that time you could almost say there was a revolution in hunting. With two major wildlife refuges within three or four hours driving distance from Kansas City, there was a boom in waterfowl hunting that was hard to believe. The Squaw Creek Wildlife Area was near Mound City, Missouri, and the Swan Lake Wildlife Area was near Minden, Missouri. Both of them were in a flyway and held heavy concentrations of ducks and geese in the early fall at migration time. Both places offered waterfowl hunting like Kansas City hunters had never dreamed of. Those who could afford it bought land around the perimeter. Landowners around the perimeters of Swan Lake and Squaw Creek leased land for duck blinds and goose pits. Some sold such land and some built their own pits and blinds to rent by the day. Almost every hunter was learning to blow a duck or goose call, or both. I joined the crowd!

I had won a Lohman call at a Ducks Unlimited Trap Shoot. I just about drove my family crazy practicing on it. The best way to learn is in the field under actual hunting conditions. I had two very good teachers, George Shaw and Harold Sankpill. George called in a lot of contests and one year made it to the World Championship contest at Stuttgart, Arkansas. Sankpill never called a contest, but in a blind he could bring in as

Sure Shot From Wyandotte

Carol Simmons, National Women's Junior Skeet Shooting Champion, October 1951.

many ducks and geese as anyone.

The State of Missouri Conservation Commission was very active in promoting waterfowl hunting. They built goose pits at Swan Lake for the public which could be rented on a name-drawing basis. They also built a smaller hunting area at the Fountain Grove Area, which was for public use. We joined the crowd and did a lot of hunting at all three areas. We also promoted it on our radio and TV shows. Kansas also had a great waterfowl shooting area at Cheyenne Bottoms near Great Bend, Kansas, and one on the Marais Des Cygne, near Pleasanton, Kansas. I have lots of wonderful memories in all the areas of both states.

Somewhere along the line I received an issue of *Prom Magazine,* published in Kansas City, Kansas. On the cover was a picture of 16-year-old Carole Simmons of Wyandotte High School. She had just won the National Skeet Shooting Championship for her age group. I thought it would be nice to honor her on my daily radio show. If I remember correctly, it was before I had my TV show. I called the school and we made the necessary arrangements. Her dad, Ernie Simmons, drove her out to Independence for the radio interview. He owned a gun shop in downtown Kansas City, Missouri, and was an avid hunter. He was an inventive genius for double-barreled guns, in the side-by-side or over and under. He invented the famous Simmons rib for shotguns, and also invented the first single trigger. That started a friendship that was special between us that lasted as long as he lived.

He not only was an avid duck hunter, but also was just as sold on his quail hunting. However, we plan to take care of the quail hunting in another section of this book. In fact, we want to share some quail and pheasant hunting, as well as some of the big game hunting. We just divided it three ways: first the waterfowl, then the upland game, and last the deer and antelope.

Getting back to the duck hunting. One September I called Ernie and asked if he wanted to go to Canada duck hunting for a few days with Dusty and me. We made the necessary arrangements and left after my TV show. We drove all night to Nestor Falls on Lake of the Woods, to Young's Wilderness Camp, where we had fished many times. Smokey, my oldest boy, was with me on the first duck-hunting expedition.

We had a great trip this year; Dusty was with me. We arrived at the camp about 3 o'clock in the afternoon. We caught our limit of small mouth bass right off the dock before we checked in. There was a group of hunters from Marshalltown, Iowa there at the same time who also had been there the year before. We had Ernie's Labrador retriever, Zoro, with us. Ernie was so proud of that dog. At dinner that night one of those hunters from Iowa asked Ernie if his Lab would retrieve a fish. Ernie said, "He probably would, but I'm afraid he might get to chasing turtles." The guy spit soup all over the table, and then laughed.

Two days later I wanted to add a shore lunch to our duck movie. We took our fishing poles out with us and soon caught enough walleye for shore lunch. They pulled the boats up on the shore and one of the native guides tossed the walleye into a small puddle of water where the waves had washed up over the rock. I happened to look around, and Zoro

Duck hunting with my friend, Ernie Simmons.

had a walleye in his mouth and was sitting, holding it for his master, just as he would a duck. I yelled for Dusty to get the camera. The dog retrieved each of those walleye. The men from Iowa were eating their sandwiches close by and saw it all. What a scene! "Wings of Chance."

The year before Smokey and I had an unusual experience! I had a friend, Glen Bowman, who owned a motel in Branson. He had done many favors for us. He had asked me several times about going on a trip with me. I called him and we made all the necessary arrangements. He drove in from Branson and joined Smokey and me. We drove all night to Nestor Falls, arriving about 3 p.m. We hunted several days with success. Then the native guide told us of a special marsh near a wild rice patch. The two boats of us made the trip. There was a floating mass of water grass, and to move on it took special care. Bowman was a big man, not fat but a big frame. After a while he said, "I can't take this."

I asked our guide if there was a beaver pond back of the woods where Bowman might hunt. We ate our sandwiches, and he took Bowman back through the woods. Smokey and I worked on the movie and did well. Late in the afternoon I began to worry, as the two of them hadn't come back. The guide was small and I knew he couldn't carry Bowman out if he had a heart attack. It grew later and I really began to worry. It was a new area to me, and I wasn't even sure Smokey and I could find them or find our way home. Just then I heard voices. I called out, and it was the two of them, each carrying his limit of mallards and his gun. I asked him if he had a problem.

He said, "Man, we went back in the woods, and soon we had mallards all over us. I shot a couple that fell and the wind blew them out of our reach. We kept waiting and hoping that some way we could retrieve the ducks. The beaver pond was not wide, but we had no way of getting to the opposite side." The wind died down and I supposed that they would throw rocks past the ducks, hoping the wake would work them back toward them. Bowman finally decided to strip off his clothes and get his ducks. He had just shed his clothes when the guide yelled that some more were circling to come into the pond. Evidently, the dead ducks served as decoys. Bowman grabbed his gun; standing stark naked he got off a couple of shots. Can you imagine what was going on in that native guide's mind? Here was a white man entirely naked, but still shooting ducks! So in two years of duck hunting in Canada we have a Labrador retriever retrieving walleye, and a naked hunter retrieving his ducks. We made several Canadian hunting trips and always enjoyed the start of another season.

We worked closely with Ducks Unlimited. In fact, for seven consecutive years we donated a national 30-minute show. They would fly us and an artist, some internationally famous, to a Ducks Unlimited project from Carrot River Project in Canada, to a project near Mexico City in Mexico. I was really impressed with the dedication and loyalty we found among the people who did the work in the field. We found that they worked hard and spent our money wisely and efficiently.

But getting back to our waterfowl hunting in the States. We had a friend, Rex Hancock, a dentist, who was an avid duck hunter. It was even said of him that he was working on a patient's tooth when his hunting buddy came by and said, "The mallards are in!" He left his patient in the chair and went duck hunting. It may not have been that bad, but it describes him perfectly. He moved to Stuttgart, Arkansas, and set up shop. I think at that time Stuttgart was the duck capital of the world. In its prime, I guess there were over a million mallards using the rice fields of the area. It may have been even more at times. Rex called me and invited me down to film the concentrations of ducks and to get in some duck hunting at the same time. I cannot recall the date, but it must have been in the early '60s. We made the necessary plans, and I drove down by myself and spent several days with him. There is no way you can describe what it was like, and it is not likely to ever be that way again.

In waterfowl hunting there is no greater sight than to see the sky full of mallards, especially in bright sunshine. God didn't paint a picture any more beautiful than that! I'm grateful that I had the opportunity to see it in its prime.

I really don't know when they started the world championship duck-calling contests; sometime in the early '60s they invited me to be one of the judges. Then, after two or three years of being a judge, they asked me to be Master of Ceremonies for the event. I did this, and just the other day I found a silver trophy with a silver flying duck which

Silver trophy given to me for being Master of Ceremonies at Stuttgart's world championship duck calling contest.

they had given me in 1968. It was a great event for the City of Stuttgart. They built a platform for the callers to perform and for the judges. If I remember correctly, it was right on Main Street, and the crowd would fill the street. A contestant qualified by winning a state calling contest, or what then was classed as winning a major contest. Kansas City sent representatives from both Kansas and Missouri. I remember at least two young men from here won the World Championship. It so happened I was Master of Ceremonies when my friend George Shaw was a contestant, and the year Bill Harper tried it, and neither of them won.

I never called in a contest, but I could bring the ducks and geese to the blind. It was all part of the thrill of waterfowl hunting. As I said earlier, I started out with a Lohman call. However, at Stuttgart a man named Chick Majors gave me two of his calls. He called them Dixie Mallard calls. They were, and still are, my favorite calls. I've been days trying to think of Chick's name. I finally thought of it in the middle of the night, got up and wrote it down, lest I not think of it again. Chick played a prominent role in the World Championship Contests in Stuttgart. Bill Harper and others in our area started making game calls. Bill is still at it near Camdenton, Missouri, but I think he produces more turkey calls than anything else. There was a flurry of waterfowl hunting in our area for several years. It then tapered off to some extent as the major river impoundments through the Dakotas, Nebraska, Kansas, Missouri and Oklahoma changed the course of the migration pattern. I think it even affected the hunting at Stuttgart. However, there is still a lot of good waterfowl shooting available, and a number of people who have waterfowl shooting clubs.

My friend, Ernie Simmons, at one time had a duck-hunting spot near the Marais Des Cygne Wildlife Refuge. He called it Pecan Grove and had me down to hunt with him many times and to shoot pictures. One day Ernie and I were in a blind together, and we had two or three days of good mallard shooting. One afternoon he said, "I'll be glad when you go home so I can shoot a hen." It was his place, but I tried to convince him to shoot only drakes. He was a good friend and made many trips with me. Ernie liked his whis-

Duck hunting with Tony Kubek, former Yankee shortstop and broadcaster, and my son-in-law, Dr. Jim Trotter, with Judge Kelso, near Nevada, Mo.

key, but never drank while he was with me. He told one of our mutual friends that going on a trip with Ensley was like joining A.A., except he didn't have meetings.

Among the baseball players I hunted with, Enos Slaughter loved waterfowl hunting more than most. I'll never forget one trip we made to my blind on upper Lake of the Ozarks. We had a good hunt; each had our limit of four mallards. When we passed through Clinton, Missouri, Enos asked me to stop at a grocery store. He came out with an empty cardboard box. He told me that he would pick the ducks as we drove home, and proceeded to go to work. I didn't pay much attention to him until he rolled down the window and tossed the down and feathers into the wind. You could hardly see back down the road. But that was Enos.

Tony Kubek, former Yankee shortstop and Yankee broadcaster, also was an avid waterfowl hunter. He called me one fall from Wisconsin and asked if I could find a good place for him and some doctor friends to camp out and hunt ducks. I called a friend of mine, Judge Kelso, who had a good duck hunting spot. Judge was a great baseball fan and was thrilled to have Tony Kubek and his friends camp at his place. We made all the necessary arrangements. What amused me was that they brought a trailer with wood and water for their camp. As if Missouri didn't have wood and water! They had a good time and shot lots of ducks and came back several more times.

When waterfowl was at its peak, there were a lot of what I would call deluxe hunting lodges. At that time, most of them were around the perimeter of Swan Lake and the

Squaw Creek Refuge. There has always been good hunting on the Missouri River, but it's a tad dangerous. Jeff Churan, a contractor at Chillicothe, Missouri, had a great spot east of Chillicothe, as did his partner. Both places had excellent lodges and great shooting areas. A salesman for Swift & Company, who at the time was one of my sponsors on TV, called me from Chicago about a goose hunting trip and wanted me to come down. He had never shot a Canada goose, and knew I hunted a lot. I called Jeff and told him about the situation. He said, "Have him come down and we will show him a good time." He flew to Kansas City and we drove him to Jeff's place. For some reason, Jeff had a conflict of schedules but said his partner would love to have us at his place. I had let on to my guest that he might have to sleep in a tent.

When we arrived at the lodge, he could hardly believe his eyes. Jeff's partner had pulled out all the stops, even bringing his private chef to cook for us. While we were there, Jeff's partner said, "Jeff and I are planning to fly to the west coast of Mexico to hunt pintails." He asked me if Dusty and I would like to make the trip to shoot a movie for my show. He owned a Beach Baron, and I thought that's going to be a long ride from here to El Paso, then across the main mountain to Cullican. He called and told me that he and Jeff had rented a Lear Jet. We flew down to Cullican, left the plane there and took a wild taxi ride to the lake. Dusty and I didn't hunt much, but I had some great bass fishing. Nothing big, but a lot of bass in the 5-6 lb. class. They had some good pintail shooting. We made a couple of movies and flew home. We lucked out on the weather.

The next week I received a call from Bud Walton, co-founder of the Wal-Mart chain. Bud and Sam and I had a lot of quail hunting together, but no waterfowl. Bud told me that his son-in-law, Sam Kroenke, wanted to hunt some ducks and geese. Once again I called Jeff. He told me that he would be delighted to have them come to his place. We made the necessary arrangements. I drove up from Kansas City to Chillicothe. Bud and Stan drove up from Versailles. We met Jeff in Chillicothe, and we took all three vehicles. Bud had his pickup and his bird dogs. Bud was more of a quail hunter and always had his dogs with him during the season. Jeff's accommodations were deluxe, but the dirt road from the highway to his lodge was a mess. It was a nasty cold day, which was fortunate, because the mud roads were frozen. We made it and were soon out in the blind. We had ducks and geese moving in and out most of the day. Right after lunch Jeff told us that he needed to get back to town. He told us to stay as long as we wanted, but to lock the lodge when we left. Late that afternoon Bud said, "I've got to let my dogs out for a while, but you two hunt till I get back." He was gone a long time and we were beginning to wonder what had happened.

It was getting late when he came back to the blind. He said, "Boys, we're in trouble. I can't start my truck." We gathered up our ducks and geese and made it back to the lodge. We tried every way to get his pickup started, but no luck. It stated to drizzle and freeze. No way could I pull him on those frozen dirt roads. Fortunately, Jeff had a telephone in the lodge. I finally reached the Ford dealer in Chillicothe, who was one of my sponsors. He told me that he didn't have a tow truck, but would call one. He asked me where I was, and the directions. We waited and waited! We saw some headlights in the distance once, but they didn't come our way. I called back to Chillicothe, and they told me the man with the tow truck got lost and needed directions again. About 9 p.m., he arrived, and he couldn't start the pickup. He told us he thought the gas line might be frozen, but he had no way to safely thaw it out. I asked him if hot water might do it. He said, "Where in the world would you get hot water?" I said, "In the lodge!" Stan and I went to the lodge. We found a bucket and came back with the hot water. He poured it on the gas line, and I'll never forget; an icicle just the size of the gas line shot out. He connected it back, and Bud started the motor. Stan and I locked up the lodge, and the three vehicles of us made it back to Chillicothe. By that time, there was ice everywhere. Bud and Stan took off for Versailles, and I for Kansas City. The icing grew worse when I came to the Missouri River on I-435; cars were stacked up with wrecks all over the place for some four or five miles, but I made it through safely to my home in Raytown. I immediately called Bud Walton's home in Versailles. Bud and Stan had just made it home. I thought of the wild trips I had made in all kinds of weather, just to hunt ducks and geese.

I have a friend in Overbrook, Kansas, Blair Flynn, who just may be the best waterfowl and quail hunter that I have ever met. Besides his hunting skills, he was one of the best fishermen for bass, crappie, hybrids, and channel catfish that I have met over the years. I have not met a more dedicated duck hunter. He called me and wanted me to come to Kansas for a fun duck hunt. I sneaked off a day from my schedule and drove to Overbrook, Kansas, where he worked for the Farmers Co-op. We then drove to Pomona Lake, pulling his boat with his decoys and boat blind. When we arrived, we set up his portable boat blind. I was amazed at how simple it was to put together. We had a tremendous mallard shoot. Blair had his Labrador retriever with him, and had a ladder on the side of the boat so the dog could climb in the boat. I was so fascinated by the ingenuity with which he had made the blind that I asked him if I could come back with Dusty and shoot a movie for my TV show.

Blair and I made many fishing and quail hunting movies over the years. He told me to do it. I told Dusty, my son, about it and he said, "Dad, boat blinds are a dime a dozen! What would be special about this one?" We set up a date with Blair and made one of the best mallard hunting shows that we had done during our 50 years.

One Monday morning Gloria, my secretary, called me about a letter we had received. Back in those days we received lots of mail, but times have changed. Gloria said, "This is a nasty letter, and you need to take care of it!" It was through the television station in Duluth, Minnesota, but was mailed from a small town in Wisconsin. I asked Gloria to read it to me. It started off: "Ensley, you're a big liar. My wife and I went to Superior, Wisconsin, to catch your seminar. We were really impressed. I asked you to come up and shoot a goose picture. You said that the public wouldn't stand still for it. Yesterday you had a duck-hunting movie. What's the difference? You're just a big liar!"

I asked Gloria to trace it down and get a phone number. I called and a lady answered the phone. I asked her if Martin Hamann was there. She called him to the phone, and I told him who I was. He said, "Ensley, you're just a big liar!" I asked him what his problem was, and he told me! I told him that to my knowledge, no one in the crowd said anything about a goose hunt, but I heard someone ask me up for a moose hunt. I told him if he wanted me for a goose hunt, just invite me this fall. I gave Martin my phone number, and in the early fall he called me.

I flew to Duluth, where he was to pick me up. He and his brother met me at the airport. They just looked like a couple of farm boys, and were! Martin and his wife milked 40 cows, and his brother worked in the timber. We stopped for breakfast in Superior, Wisconsin. They told me that they needed to stop at a sporting goods store and get me a license. I told them that I was going to be on camera taking pictures. They told me they were going to buy my license; they wanted me to shoot some. When I saw they were serious, I said, "You're not going to pay for my license." So I paid for it. They were nice young men, and we had a chance to get acquainted as we drove to their homes near the little town of Mason, Wisconsin. I asked Martin if there was a motel there where I could stay. He said, "No, you are going to stay with me." When we arrived at his place, it was a two-room trailer home. I asked him where I was going to sleep. He told me in their bedroom. I asked him where he and his wife were going to sleep; he told me in the kitchen on a rollaway. He told me that he and his wife had to milk at 4 a.m., but that I could sleep a little longer. I began to wonder what I had gotten myself into.

The next morning, after an early breakfast, I asked Martin where we were going to hunt. He said, "On the neighbor's joining our land." He has a clover field next to a cornfield. The geese have been working that field. We drove the short distance to the neighbor's farm. He gave us permission to hunt, but said that he would like us to use his 12-year-old boy in the picture. He brought out an old rusty shotgun and gave it to the boy. Martin had a shovel, his shotgun and some goose decoys.

We walked out in the clover field and Martin dug a trench about 18 inches deep, 3 foot wide and 6 foot long. He put a tarp in the trench and had the boy lie down in it. I asked Martin if the kid had ever fired a gun. Martin said, "I don't know." I said, "Get him out of there before he shoots himself!" I asked him if he had a hatchet or a small handsaw. He got a hatchet; we cut some brush and made a good makeshift blind. He put the decoys out, and in short order we started calling geese to the decoys. I do not remember if the boy shot a goose or not, but we had a great hunt. For three days we had geese all over us and made the movie for my TV show. The local newspaper sent a photographer out to do a story. Everyone in the community was excited about it. Martin and his family became family to me. He and his wife drove me to Duluth to catch a plane home.

That evening after I came home I received a call from Martin. He just wanted to see if I made it home safely. In a short week of goose hunting we built a friendship that has lasted all these years. A wonderful friendship that would not have happened but for a misunderstanding and a letter. "Wings of Chance."

It seemed different to mix hunting of waterfowl, upland game and big game into the same arena. I decided to split the book, divided somewhat equally, with the three categories. I spent most of the early part of the book about waterfowl hunting during my broad-

Ernie Simmons, the famous gun-smith, with his daughter Carol and son Junior.

casting years. Now we want to savor the special moments of upland hunting.

As I mentioned earlier, as a boy in western Kansas there were no quail or pheasant, only prairie chickens. I shot my first quail in Oklahoma, but didn't really get with the program until we moved to Independence, Missouri. Years before, some friends brought me my first shotgun. It was almost an antique, a 12-gauge model 13 Winchester. It had a fairly open bore, and I shot well with it. I thought that if I could buy a good shotgun, I could do better. I bought a Browning 12-gauge auto-loader from my friend, Ernie Simmons. It must not have fit me properly because I shot so poorly! I was embarrassed to hunt with anyone.

I bought my wife a 12-gauge J.C. Higgins repeating shotgun with an adjustable cuts compensator. She wanted to learn to quail hunt. She had never shot a shotgun and I thought she would never learn! We bought a couple of bird dogs and started to work on it. There were lots of quail then and plenty of places to hunt. I got progressively worse and Bonnie got better. I called my friend, Ernie Simmons, to see if I could do a quail story for television with him, his son J.R. and his daughter Carol. It was to be a father, son and daughter quail hunt. I knew that all of them were good shooters. It pleased Ernie, and we arranged a date and a place. The weather cooperated. We found lots of birds and made the movie. We still had some time, and Ernie insisted that I shoot a few birds. I told him that my gun was back at the car. He handed me his 28-gauge Remington and

Quail hunting with Buddy Baier and Enos Slaughter.

said, "Use this." I had been doing so poorly with the Browning 12-gauge that I was almost embarrassed to try it in front of them. You will not believe it, but I dropped eight straight quail without missing. I turned to Ernie and asked him what he wanted for the gun. He wanted to know why. I told him I wanted to buy it! He said, "Since it's you, I'll sell it for $85." I bought the gun, and it opened up a whole new world of quail hunting.

We bought a Pointer bird dog and named him Country Squire. Ford, at that time, was my sponsor on television. We took Country Squire with us almost everywhere. He soon became a legend of his own, because we used him on so many TV shows.

Early in my TV years I received a telephone call from a man named Charlie Sandlin, who asked me if I would help a young couple at Peculiar, Missouri. He told me that they had just moved here from Texas and started a shooting preserve and needed help. It was the first shooting preserve in this part of the country. They featured quail, pheasant and Chukkar partridges. Their names were Buddy and Denny Baier. They called it Baier's Den Kennels and Shooting Preserve. Buddy was a professional dog trainer and boarded the dogs. It was my first hunting movie for television. The Baiers became like family to me and my family, and he has remained that way until this day, 48 years later. I was so proud of our Country Squire that I asked Buddy to let Squire sire a litter of pups. He did and raised a fine bunch of puppies. We had a friend who loved to hunt but didn't have money to buy a dog, so Bonnie and I gave him one of the males. While the pup was still young, he and his brothers shot over him with 12-gauge shotguns. The dog became gun-shy and even bird-shy. Later, he also got mange. He gave the dog to Bonnie's dad, saying the dog was no good. Bonnie's dad was in his 70s and lived on 40 acres in South Missouri, near the little town of Stella. He had a covey of quail on his place and, of course, knew all the neighbors, who would let him hunt. He fed the dog and cured the mange. Almost every day he would take the dog around his place. He was slow and could hardly keep up with the dog. He seldom was close enough to the birds to shoot; therefore he and the pup worked patiently together.

Meanwhile, my wife, Bonnie, was having problems hitting quail. I learned one thing about teaching people. If a person has a strong desire to learn, they can do it. Bonnie wanted so much to become a good quail shot that she made it. I would go on a speaking trip, and she would take the dogs and drive down and hunt with her dad. Usually, when I finished my night's work, I would call to see how the day's hunt went. At first when I called her and asked how she and her dad did, she would say that both of them shot their limit, one apiece, and we would laugh about it. I asked her where they hunted. She told me that they hunted on her dad's place and got up five coveys. I later found out that they flushed the same covey five times! All the neighbors would let them hunt because they never hurt the birds. This went on for two years. Bonnie came in one time from hunting with her dad. She said, "You must go down sometime and see what that Squire dog is doing." Finally I did! The dog pointed and held more birds than my fancy dogs. I couldn't believe it. The old man, with patience and kindness, had cured a dog that was gun-shy and bird-shy. When her dad got too old to hunt, I bought the dog. I used him on television for several years. That was 40 years ago, and I still have people say, "I still remember Country Squire." He was a dog that was practically given up for dead and became a TV star!

I had Buddy raise another litter of puppies and got another Squire dog. When the pup was almost a year old, I asked Buddy about making a movie of him training the young Squire. We arranged a date in the early fall. It was a beautiful day when I drove out to Buddy's. In fact, it was a little on the warm side when we started working the dog. I had to stop and load my camera. While I was loading the camera, Buddy told the boy who was helping us to take the dog a short distance to a small stream that ran through the pasture to get the dog a drink. I told Buddy that I was ready to finish the movie. The boy had not come back with the dog. Buddy yelled, "I didn't want you to teach him to swim, just give him a drink and get back here!" You have to know Buddy to appreciate his wit.

Buddy and Denny took care of dogs for years, and we hunted and fished together. I was, at that time, master of ceremonies at the Denver Sport Show, and also at Wichita and Tulsa. I would take Buddy with me to promote his place. We had a special friendship. It all started with my first movie on television of shooting pheasants on his shooting preserve, and with a stranger, Charlie Sandlin, a viewer and a friend of the Baiers. We lost track of him, but our friendship with the Baiers goes on and on.

I must tell you one more story about Buddy. He trained dogs for wealthy customers who wanted to hunt woodcock. This bird migrated through this region, but you seldom saw them. Occasionally, we would shoot one during the early part of quail season. Buddy wanted to know if I knew of a place where we might have a good hunt. He told me that this man had a Beach Baron and would fly us wherever we needed to go. I called my friend, Bill Hall, who operated a hunting and fishing camp at Pendleton Bridge on Toledo Bend Reservoir in Louisiana. I told him of my problem. He told me the timing was

15

right, for the woodcock had just moved in. He told me he had a friend who was the state biologist who would work with us. We set it up to fly down New Year's Day, if the weather was right. Buddy said that we would plan to leave at noon; then he called me and said that the man wanted to watch part of the football game. I immediately told Buddy that I didn't like the idea of flying into that little airport at Many, Louisiana, after dark. I was really concerned about it. Dusty and I drove to Kansas City's Executive Field. When we arrived there, I saw a Beach Baron just outside the hangar. I supposed it was his plane. Then they rolled a new Executive North American jet out. He said to me, "What do you think of my new airplane?" It almost bowled me over with surprise. I told him that we could not land at Many, Louisiana, in that plane. He told me that he didn't intend to, that we were going to land at Lake Charles, Louisiana, rent a car and drive to Toledo Bend. We did, but didn't arrive at Bill Hall's place until late that night. He, Dusty, and Buddy had two good days of woodcock hunting with Bill and his biologist friend. I didn't join them, for I wanted to fish, although I brought my duck gun with me just in case the mallards would arrive by then.

The night before the last day, Bill told us to get up early and drive to his "pet" duck hunting spot on the Gulf Coast near Lake Charles, Louisiana. That's the nice thing about duck hunting, you normally have to get up early to get with the program. We made it to Bill's spot early morning, and with hip-waders we waded out to his blinds. The mud in the marsh was terrible. You could hardly wade through it. At that time, I was running 5-6 miles a day. I thought I was in pretty good physical condition, but that mud was something else. Each of us carried our shotguns and some shells. It was at least 200 yards from the road, and by the time we got to the blind we were really sapped. Dusty and Bill made it to their blind, while Buddy, his friend and I made it to ours. It was a blue bird day. We hadn't seen a duck flying anywhere. About 11 a.m. we saw two local ducks swinging our way. I started calling, and the two ducks started to our decoys. I told Buddy that the ducks might not move in close, but if we wanted any ducks we had better try these two. I had my 12-gauge, Model 11 mag with three-inch shells. Buddy had his side-by-side 20 with Magnum loads, and his friend had a 28-gauge quail gun, which he had been using to hunt woodcock. I said, "Buddy, let's take them. They're as close as they're going to come." The ducks were out there about 30 yards and about 15 yards high. We all three stood up and fired. Both ducks fell about 60 yards out. Buddy's friend, with his quail gun, said, "Man, I didn't know this 28 would shoot this far." Buddy, without a moment's hesitation, called the guy by name and said, "Why don't you go pick up your ducks?" He stepped out of the blind and started toward the ducks. In that terrible sticky mud he could only go a short distance, and then stop to rest. The wind was blowing the ducks a little farther away. He finally reached the ducks and started back to the decoys and stopped to rest. Buddy almost fell off the blind seat laughing!

I said, "What is the matter with you?" He said, "When he stopped in the decoys, I thought about yelling, hey, lookout, alligator; but I thought he might have a heart attack." That was a typical Buddy Baier observation. I could almost fill a book with just Buddy's sayings; he said so many great lines. It didn't make any difference where we were: hunting, fishing, or working the sports shows in Denver, Tulsa, or Wichita, Buddy's wit kept everyone entertained. "Wings of Chance."

In the late '30s my dad and mom moved from the dust of western Kansas to Bentonville, Arkansas. I'm not sure of the date, but we were visiting them on a regular basis. My mother kept telling me that I should meet a man named Sam Walton, who had just opened a Ben Franklin Store on the square in Bentonville. She said, "He is the nicest man, and his oldest boy, Rob, throws my paper." Mother was den mother for the Cub Scouts, and, if I remember correctly, Rob had been one of them. One Saturday when we were visiting

Dusty and his Brittany, Duke.

Dad and Mom, she asked me if I would take her to the Ben Franklin Store to buy some thread. Mom did a lot of sewing, and I was glad for an opportunity to help her. I drove her down to the store, and she introduced me to Sam Walton.

This turned out to be a big moment in my life. Mom bought the thread while Sam and I talked about hunting. Sam was an avid quail hunter. We talked about our bird dogs and planned a hunt together. I'm not sure where we did our first hunt together. It started a friendship that lasted as long as he lived. He and his brother Bud founded the Wal-Mart stores with their first one at Rogers, Arkansas. It too is an amazing story, as it is now a global operation. We had some great hunts with Sam, and later with him and Bud.

Sam called me from Bentonville and asked Dusty and me to come to Claremore, Oklahoma, for a hunt with him and Bud. He had his pilot, Bill, pick us up in Kansas City and flew us down. We put our dogs on the plane and joined Sam and Bud at Claremore. We hunted on Helen Walton's dad's place, and, if I remember correctly, her dad was in his 90s. He still owned a bird dog and might have hunted with us for a while. We had a real good hunt, shot a picture, and Bill flew us back to Kansas City. A few years later Sam called me about a hunt. He had some banker friends from Chicago that he wanted to entertain. Bud was going to drive up to join us, and everyone else would fly up. It was just before Christmas, but the weather was nice, although cold. We met near Manhattan, Kansas, and had two days of good hunting.

The third day, along in mid-afternoon, Sam asked me if he could use my station wagon. He wanted to visit the Wal-Mart store in Manhattan. I told him I needed to see a friend there. We started in, stopped at a café in a small town for a bite, and then I asked Sam to drive. We arrived at the Manhattan store. Sam pulled up in the fire lane. He said, "I want everyone to know you're here."

I always drove a red Ford Country Sedan with my name on it. We went into the store, and he introduced me to the manager and the employees. Later, two young men walked up to me and asked if the dogs in the car were mine. We visited for a while. They were students at Kansas State University, and they had watched my TV show through the years. One of them, Larry North, asked me if we needed a place to hunt. He told me his mother owned 3,000 acres near Council Grove, Kansas. That was not far from where we had been hunting. They gave me their phone number and told me to call if we needed a place to hunt. Then they went on their way.

Sam came up and said, "We can still make the store in Junction City before it closes, if you don't mind." I told him that he was the driver and I was ready. It was near closing time when we reached the Junction City store. We both had on our ragged hunting clothes. Much of the help was military, and most of them didn't recognize either of us. We walked through the store to sporting goods. The young associate behind the counter didn't know either of us. There was pegboard hanging back of the counter with just two dog whistles on it. Sam said, "Sonny, we want 12 whistles on there at all times." We located the manager, who took Sam through the store.

We drove back to the motel in the town near where we were hunting. We hunted the next day until noon. Sam and his guests flew back to Bentonville. Bud and I stayed to hunt that afternoon. Late that afternoon Bud said, "Let's drive into Council Grove. There's a famous eating place there, and I'll buy you a big steak!"

As we pulled up in front of the place to park, the two young men that Sam and I met the night before walked across the street in front of us. I said, "Bud, those are the boys who told me they had access to 3,000 acres of good quail hunting territory here just east of town. Bud said, "Call them back. We may want to hunt there tomorrow. I'll buy their dinner!" I called to them and we had dinner together. I asked them if they might want to hunt with us the next day. They did.

Bud and I met them for breakfast the next morning. We drove out to Larry's mother's place, less than five miles from the city. It was a great place to hunt, and we had a great time. Larry invited us back anytime we wanted to hunt, and Bud and I did go back several times. If Sam hadn't wanted to visit the Wal-Mart store in Manhattan, we probably would never have met those two fine young men, with some great quail hunting spots. "Wings of Chance."

A year later, Sam and Bud met Dusty and me southwest of Topeka to shoot a quail movie for TV. Both of them brought their dogs, all pointers. I had County Squire, my pointer, a pretty little setter, and Dusty had his Brittany. When we let the dogs out, Sam saw Dusty's Brittany for the first time. He said, "Dusty, what are you doing with that short-tailed dog?" Bud said, "Little Brother, don't say any more about that short-tailed dog until you have seen him work." Dusty's Brittany matched the pointer stride for stride for three days, and Sam was convinced. Sam and Bud were both good hunters and good shots.

Sam called from Bentonville and said that he had some hunting buddies from Texas who wanted to hunt pheasant for a few days. He had made arrangements for a place to hunt near Hiawatha, Kansas. He wanted me to bring my dogs and help him entertain them. He gave me the date and I met them there. The first day he put me with two of his friends from Texas. It was a miserable day with a wet snow falling. We had a good hunt, but came to the motel that night wet and cold. I think our party bought all of the cold-weather gear that they had in the Wal-Mart store.

At dinner that night Sam asked me why I was shooting my wife's 20-gauge instead of my 28. I told them that 28-gauge shells were hard to come by. I told him that I had a friend who had promised to get me some 28-gauge shells, but it hadn't happened. Sam didn't say any more about the shells, but told the boys that they had hunted with me that day; however, he and I were going to hunt together the next day. The next day when I sat down at the table to eat with the crew, I found three boxes of Federal 28-gauge shells by my plate. It was a special project from Federal. Each shell had Sam Walton's name on it. I still have them. No way was I going to use them. Sam and I hunted that day and had a good shoot. They flew back to Bentonville, and I drove home with some fond memories and three boxes of Sam Walton souvenirs.

I must tell you one more Sam Walton story. Sam had a lease on a big quail hunting area. I had been his guest on several occasions. He called me and asked me if I would like to meet him and Bud at Bentonville, to fly down to his Texas lease with a couple of others to hunt and shoot a quail hunting movie. I met them at the airport, and we flew down with the dogs in his twin-engine plane. Bud rode co-pilot to College Station in Texas, where we took a break and refueled. When we started to leave, Bud said his legs were tired and asked me to ride up front with Sam. It was a gorgeous day. As soon as we were airborne, Sam put the plane on automatic pilot. He said, "Harold, you keep watching for planes; I want to answer my mail." He pulled out a bag of letters and started making notes on them. We made it safely to our destination and had some real good days of quail shooting.

When we started to leave, Sam got the weather report. He said a bad cold front was moving in from the north. He called Bill, his pilot in Bentonville, and asked him to fly to Houston and meet us there. Sam at that time did not have an instrument rating. We met Bill in Houston just before dark. As we took off, Bud was up front with Bill, and Sam said, "Boys, now is the time to start to clean our quail." We started cleaning birds. We hit the cold front about halfway to Texarkana. It started hard and the air was bouncing us around, dogs and all! After a ways Sam said, "Bill, I think we better set down in Texarkana, rent a car and drive home."

However, the storm abated some. Bill said, "Sam, I think we can make it to Fort Smith." Bill checked the weather at Fayetteville. He said, "I think we can make it to Fayetteville." We made it to Fayetteville. Bill checked the weather at Rogers. He said, "Sam, we can't land at Bentonville, but we can make it to Rogers." We did. I got a kick out of Sam's farmer friend when he stepped off the plane. He said, "Harold, I feel like Santa Claus. I never looked down so many chimneys in my life." I asked Sam why he didn't get his instrument rating. The next week I called the home office and asked for Sam. They told me that he was in Florida working on his instrument flying to get his license.

I flew to Texas to hunt a few years later. When we were landing at the airport, Sam said, "Bud, I'm going to bunk with Harold. You can stay with the other guys." Sam contracted cancer, as did my wife, Bonnie. When we would meet at the stockholders' meeting, Sam would always look up Bonnie. They would compare notes as to their progress. They passed away just a few weeks apart. If my mom hadn't wanted to buy some thread, I might never have met Sam Walton! "Wings of Chance."

2

I HAVE LOVED dogs since I was a little boy. Whenever a stray dog came by our ranch, I took it in. My earliest memory of dogs is a shepherd we called Shep; a small duke's mixture dog we named Ted; and a three-legged dog named Houndy. I must have driven my parents out of their minds, for these three dogs were at my side constantly. If I went hunting, they followed me; if I went fishing, they followed. They had a passion for hunting snakes. When they found one, they would circle it until the snake would strike at one of them. Then one of the others would grab the snake and kill it. When they found a rattlesnake, they gave a different bark than when they found a non-poisonous one. However, eventually each one of the three got hit with a rattler. Shep died from hers, but the other two managed to live through the ordeal.

My dad used to winter cattle for the Liggett Cattle Company out of Andover, Kansas. They would ship the cattle by rail from Wichita to Healy, a small town in western Kansas. Then they would drive them to our ranch. Dad would feed and pasture them through the winter. He fed the cattle hay and cottonseed cake. It is hard for me to believe that cottonseed cake was available in those early years. However, I remember that Dad would leave some land for winter pasture. The prairie was covered with dense buffalo grass. It had a dense growth, but didn't get much height. It was rich in nutrients, whether the

Feeding the puppies started a love for dogs that I have never lost.

growing season or during its winter dormant time. I can still see my dad as he would scatter small piles of cottonseed cake across the pasture, and the cattle would follow. I'm sure that God made the buffalo grass to support the multitude of buffalo herds that once roamed the prairie. It was amazing that, after these herds were destroyed, you could find buffalo horns on the prairie. And I remember helping harvest wheat in the summertime. There would still be spots in the field that they called buffalo wallows. In those small wallows the wheat would thrive better than the rest of the land. I can remember helping my dad break sod with a team and a plow. Actually, it was virgin land. Then came the dust bowl years, and buffalo grass practically disappeared. Two young men at Healy, Kansas, Gerald and Gayle Sharp, started a grass seed company, which exists to this day. They traveled about the west combining buffalo grass and other prairie grasses. It's an amazing story, but I must get back to my dogs.

One fall, when the Liggetts shipped the cattle to our place, they brought a shepherd dog. It was to be a great cattle dog to work the cattle, as a sheep dog would work a herd of sheep. However, the dog was supposed to be dangerous around children. I was told not to go near the dog. After its work, Dad would tether it in one of the small shacks near the barn that was used as farrowing pens for hogs. It wasn't many days until I started sneaking table scraps out to the dog. The dog and I became friends. I finally got up enough courage to get inside the shack and started petting the dog. Mom and Dad were not aware of this for a while. However, you cannot fool your mom for long. Out of curiosity she followed me at a distance when I was carrying some table scraps. She nearly passed out when she saw me get in the shack with that dog. She started to pull me out, but the dog wouldn't let her touch me. You can imagine how that went over with Mom! I found out when we got to the house!! However, after that they decided to let the dog run free when he was not working cattle, and he was by my side constantly. One day my sister, who was older, was upset over something I had done and started to grab me. That dog chased her to the house. Mom came out with the switch, but that dog quickly sent her back to the house. The end result was that I couldn't stay out of the house forever. Mom took care of the situation properly, and I never had that dog chase my sister after that. Nobody could believe how protective that dog was of me. It was a sad day for a little boy when the owners came for their cattle and their dog. I can still see the look on Mom's face when that dog refused to let her use that switch on me. "Wings of Chance," that one of the dogs I loved most as a youngster was not my own!

There were no quail or pheasant in our part of the country, so no pointers or setters that I remember. The coyote hunters had greyhounds, but I never owned one. I can remember as a youngster the little town of Shields, Kansas, and what they called an annual picnic. It was quite an attraction, with a carnival, baseball games and the lake. They drew people from a radius of 40 or 50 miles. I can vaguely remember their greyhound races. They would fasten a pulley to the rear wheel of a Model T Ford. They would then jack up the one wheel and fasten a wire around the pulley. They would stretch the wire across the level prairie ground for several hundred yards and tie on a small bundle of burlap sacks. I think they would race only two greyhounds at a time. They would crank up the old Model T, and the pulley on the rear wheel would wind the wire, pulling the object as though it were a rabbit. The dogs then raced after it. I do not know if that was the start of the greyhound racing we have today, but it may have been something like that. Sounds

Darwin Stewart, my high school buddy, and his daughter, Lee Mae, and his greyhound.

pretty corny! Wings of Chance!" I never owned a greyhound, but I understand that they can be made into good pets.

My high school chum, Darwin Stewart, became an avid coyote hunter. We both lettered in three sports and our senior year advanced to the semi-finals in the Kansas State High School Championship Tennis games at Manhattan, Kansas. Healy was just a small school, but at that time there was no classification of schools, so we had to compete against the large schools. However, getting back to Darwin and his coyote hunting. Some 45 years later, some friends of mine and I drove to my hometown to hunt pheasants with Darwin. You couldn't hunt pheasants until noon, so he took us coyote hunting one morning. He had a 1934 Ford with the back seat out. He put the greyhounds in the back, and

Darwin Stewart, my high school chum, daughter Lee Mae and proof of his coyote hunting skills.

we took off. I'll never forget that ride. One of my buddies was back with the dogs, and he won't forget it either! The dogs were all over him and even licking his face. The territory we hunted was on the south slope of the Smokey Hill Valley. You would never believe where he put that Ford. We went up and down hills, across canyons, eroded areas and grassy gulleys. We saw several coyotes, but never caught one. That afternoon we had some good pheasant hunting, even on the old home place. We had a good time, but my friends from Missouri will not forget their first coyote hunt with greyhounds in a 1934 Ford. It would be a different story today, with four-wheel drive vehicles.

I've heard it said that you can't have a good hunting dog and make a house pet of it! I don't know where that idea came from, but it surely wasn't from hunters. I have known a lot of good hunters who owned excellent bird dogs and kept them in the house as pets. Sam and Bud Walton both had great dogs that were pets. Nearly everyone remembers Sam's setter, Ol' Roy. I think Audie Walton told me that Bud's favorite dog, a pointer, was called Jake.

My son Dusty has had two of the finest Brittanys that I ever shot over. The first one he called Duke, and the other he called Covey. They were both house pets. I called my friend, Blair Flynn, of Overbrook, Kansas. We have hunted and fished together for 40 years. He may be one of the best all-around hunters and fishermen that I've met in my lifetime. I asked him the question. His answer, "I have never seen a great bird dog that wasn't also a great pet." I've seen a lot of great retrieving dogs that were great pets. I shot my first quail in Oklahoma some 60 years ago. I bought my first bird dog some 50 years ago in Missouri. It was a female pointer named Patsy, and she cost $50. In today's market Patsy would be good enough to bring thousands. She was truly a great dog and a great pet. Probably my most famous dogs were male pointers. We raised Country Squire and Country Squire, Jr. They have been gone some 25 years, and I still have people ask about them. It seems that people remember three things about my TV series: my red Ford Country Sedan, County Squire, my bird dog, and my theme song, "Gone Fishin'." However, the greatest hunting dog and the greatest pet of them all was my last dog, a male setter whose registered name was Wendy's Ben, but to me it was always just plain Ben Dog, and I must tell you about Ben.

One September, some 20 years ago, my daughter Sandy and her husband, Dr. Jim Trotter, met me at the airport in Kansas City. A group of us had just returned from our annual movie-making trip to Costa Rica. My birthday was coming up in November, and Sandy said, "Dad, Jim and I have a surprise for your coming birthday. We have bought the pick-of-the-litter of setter puppies. The puppies are about five or six weeks old. We are to take you out to Blue Springs, Missouri, this week for you to make your choice." It is a day I'll never forget! The people who owned the puppies invited us into their home. They had spread a blanket on the living room floor and placed the eight setter puppies on it. The puppies were all sleeping when we came in. However, one puppy awakened and stood on its feet, with its tail straight up. It went "Bow-wow-wow," as if to challenge our presence. I said, "If that's a male, that's my pick!" It was a male, and from that day on there was a bond between Ben Dog and me that will last in my memory as long as I live. Thousands of families have pets that have become part of the family, but there is something extra-special about a good hunting dog. Ben went through his puppy stage, as most dogs do, endearing himself to us more every day. We have a large fenced-in back yard with about a third of it in garden. Ben roamed the yard and garden at will. I started working with him as a puppy with a bird wing on a string. It was just natural for him to start pointing. I'm not so sure that you can teach a dog to point. They either have the

Ben Dog on his first point on a quail wing in my back yard.

instinct to do it, or not. I suppose some dogs have more talent than others. Ben appeared to have it all! As he grew, he played around the yard and garden, pointing grasshoppers, and about anything that moved. I had planted a row of gladiolas across the garden. When they started blooming, an occasional bumble bee would find them. Ben would point them and then try to catch them. That must have been a big surprise when he got one in his mouth, for he really would shake his head! I had planted a row of sugar-snap peas and put up a chicken wire fence for them to climb. By this time Ben was almost grown. One day I noticed him picking the pods and eating them. It was hard for me to understand how a dog could tell the pod from the vine, but Ben did, and he never destroyed the plants. As long as Ben lived, I planted a row of sugar-snap peas for him. I continued to work with him on his pointing, using a bird wing.

November came and with it the opening of quail season. I knew it was time to get Ben used to a gun, but you have to do it carefully. I have seen good bird dogs ruined by shooting over them before they are ready. When the quail season opened on a warm November day with a bright sun shining, my late wife, Bonnie, and I put Ben in that red Ford Country Sedan. We drove about 50 miles to a friend's farm near Pomona Lake. I asked him if I could take my young dog out to get him used to a gun. I told him that I didn't want to shoot any birds, just get the dog started with me in the field. He gave us permission but said, "If you find some birds and need to, just go ahead and shoot." No one was living on the place, so we drove out into the pasture and parked. I had my .22 rifle and my 28-gauge shotgun with me. I told Bonnie to stay in the car with Ben and that I would take the rifle and walk away. I wanted Ben to see me with a gun. Ben had a fit that he couldn't go along. I repeated the process and left Ben in the car. Ben was really wanting out of the car to go with me. I wanted him to associate being with me when I was carrying a gun. Each time when I reached a certain distance, I would fire a shot with the .22 rifle. Hunting dogs learn to associate a gun with a good time. You can take any good hunting dog, inside the house or out in the yard, and handle a gun,

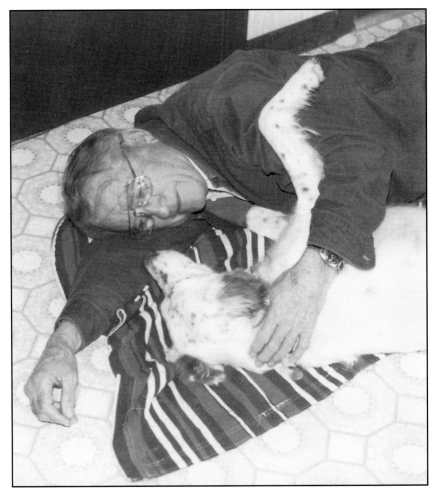

Ben Dog, my all-time favorite hunting dog and house pet.

and that dog will get excited. When I thought Ben was excited enough, Bonnie and I let him out. We walked down a draw and around the pasture. Ben was really happy. He finally came down on a point in some grass. We walked over to him and stood there for a short time. Ben never moved. I was hoping it was a quail, but it was a grasshopper. I petted Ben a few times and kicked the grasshopper up and fired the rifle into the air. Ben never flinched, and I knew I was on the right track. We worked Ben around the pasture awhile, but found no birds. I told Bonnie that we needed to find a place where there was some quail. We went back to the car and started driving through the countryside.

After passing several farms, we came to what I thought might be a good place to start. I drove into the driveway and went to the door to ask for permission to work my young dog. A lady came to the door, and I told her why I was there. She looked out and saw my red Country Sedan with my name on it. She exclaimed, "You're Harold Ensley! Let me call my husband!" She invited me in and I met him. I told him that I was training my young setter pup. He told me that he didn't hunt, but had seen several coveys of quail on his place and that I was certainly welcome to hunt. He told me that I could come back anytime to hunt, but I must always ask permission. He told me that if they didn't happen to be there, just leave a note on the front door and go ahead and hunt. However, if you don't ask permission, when I hear shooting, "I'll run you off my place." I told him that I never hunted anyplace without asking permission, and I really appreciated the favor.

Bonnie and I drove to the field he suggested and parked the wagon. I told Bonnie that I was going to carry my shotgun, just in case we found some quail. When Ben saw me get the gun, he really wanted out. We let him out and he really started hunting. We had walked about 30 minutes when Ben went on a beautiful point, with his tail high. I really thought it might be a grasshopper. I kept talking to Ben; I walked up and petted him for a moment, when out came a covey of quail. I was so startled that I didn't shoot for a moment. I was so close to Ben that I thought that I might scare him, but finally did shoot and got one bird. Ben didn't even flinch at the sound of the gun. It was Ben's first covey point and the first quail killed over him. It was a happy time for both of us. Bonnie and I together hunted and worked Ben.

It was getting late in the afternoon when we started back to the station wagon. Ben didn't want to quit, but I finally got him into his crate. During the process, I had put my gun down in the grass in order to get Ben by the collar. We started driving home and were almost there when I thought of my shotgun. I asked Bonnie if I had put it in the wagon. She said that she didn't remember. I pulled off the highway, checked the car, and no gun! I had left it on the ground at the edge of the field. I thought about driving back

Ben Dog on point in the back yard.

Ben Dog on point in the field.

to look for it, but decided to go on home and get it the next day.

Early the next morning I loaded Ben in the station wagon and headed back to get the gun. I was hoping that the men who were combining beans had not run over it. When I reached the spot, the gun was there. I decided that I would drive to the farmhouse to ask permission to hunt again. There was no one home, so I decided to write a note telling them that I was hunting. Do you think I could find a pencil or paper in my wagon? No way! I drove to a neighbor's place a few miles away and they were not home.

I had a hunting and fishing buddy, Blair Flynn, who lived at Overbrook, Kansas. Blair ran the tire and battery operation for the co-op there. Blair liked to hunt. It was only a few miles out of my way, so I stopped to see if he could go with me. Blair knew all the farmers and had plenty of places to hunt. I showed him Ben, my new dog, and asked him if we could find a place to hunt. Blair was a great duck hunter, as well as being a great quail hunter. His knees had started giving him some trouble. He said, "Harold, I'd rather hunt duckies," as he called them. "I can call them to me, but you have to walk for those quailey birds." I told him I just wanted to shoot some birds over my young dog. He consented to go. It was a beautiful November day and he wasn't too busy. He told me of a farmer friend who had invited him out, saying that he had seen four or five coveys on his place. His crops were still in the field and the cover was heavy, but Blair and I thought we could find enough birds to work Ben. We had just about covered the place, and the day had warmed up. Blair said, "I told you about this walking bit; I would rather hunt ducks!" However, he said that he knew of another farm not too far away. We drove there and started hunting. Ben pointed a covey and several singles. We had some good shooting. Ben pointed well and retrieved well. Blair said, "Ensley, you have the markings of a great bird dog. I know of another place we should try." We did, and finished out our limit of birds.

On the way back to Overbrook, Blair asked me if I could bring the dog back and hunt

Saturday. He had some special spot he wanted to try. He said, "While you have the pup progressing, let's just really break him in right." Ben and I drove back to Blair's on Saturday. He took us to that special spot. It was a day to be remembered. Ben pointed five or six coveys and lots of singles. Blair said, "That dog has an uncanny sense of finding coveys. He's got it made now. It is just a matter of shooting lots of birds over him." That we did. We later shot several movies for our TV series, and Ben became a real star and one of my best pals. I'm talking about the bond between a hunter and his favorite dog.

Ben loved to hunt, and he loved to travel. He loved to stay in the house, and he loved the garden. He had a constant battle with the bumble bees around the flowers. I always raised a big garden. If I had a hobby, it would be a race between gardening and jogging. To me, the person who has never planted a seed and watched the plant as it grows to maturity to bear fruit has missed something in life. It's one of God's many great miracles that are with us constantly.

One year my daughter Sandy asked me to plant some jalapeno peppers. She wanted to make some jalapeno jelly. I love sweet peppers and almost always raise a few plants. However, that spring I put out a few plants just for Sandy. The plants did well. One day my six-year-old grandson, David, and I were digging to get a few worms to catch bluegill. David looked over and saw the peppers. There were probably a dozen peppers that had ripened and were a bright red. He said, "Grandpa, can I eat one of those?" I told him that he could. He picked one and took a big bite. It must have set him on fire, for he started screaming, "Nanna, Nanna, bring me some water!" He always called Bonnie Nanna. Ben Dog was standing by. He looked at David, and then looked at me, as though asking if he could have one. Then he proceeded to eat five or six of those hot peppers and never batted an eye.

One day David and I were digging worms at the edge of the asparagus patch where we occasionally found a big night-crawler in with the regular worms. This crawler was writhing like a snake, and David was afraid to pick it up. I said, "David, pick up that worm!" He said, "No, Grandpa!" I told him a second time, and he refused. I said, "David, pick up that worm and put it in the can. If you don't, I'll get your little sister Leslee to pick it up." David then picked up the night-crawler and put it in the can. A short time later we found another big night-crawler. David didn't want to touch it. I told him again that if he didn't do it I would go get Leslee. He said, "Why don't you go get Leslee?" I had pushed him as far as he wanted to go.

I have one more garden story I want to share with you. For years I have raised Burpees burpless cucumbers. I would plant them near a wire trellis and let them climb. I've had the plants grow as high as 12 or 14 feet. A few years ago, I was preparing to go to Canada to shoot movies for my TV show. My tomatoes were just starting to color, and my cucumber plants had climbed to about 10 feet high. The vines were loaded with tiny cucumbers. I figured that they would be ready to pick when I returned. When we returned, I could hardly wait to get down to the garden for a fresh tomato and cucumber. The tomatoes were there, but not a cucumber was there! I just assumed that Jeanne, the lady who takes care of my medicine, etc., had picked them. She comes in Monday through Friday and takes care of things. She also did the print-out of my first book on the computer. I asked her if she had picked the cucumbers while I was gone. She told me no, that perhaps Dwain Paugh, a fishing buddy of mine, might have picked them. I called Dwain. He said that he didn't do it, that maybe Jeanne had picked them. We just couldn't figure out what had happened to them. A few days later, I was sitting on a bench in the shade looking down toward the garden. I saw a beautiful red male cardinal fly into the cucumber vines. Then it dawned on me that this bird was the culprit! However, in all my years of gardening I had never seen any bird eat a cucumber! I have a nylon netting that I use to cover my strawberry patch. I took the netting and put it around the cucumber vines. It wasn't 30 minutes before a male cardinal had flown into the vine and was trapped. I rescued the bird without harm and released it. Now I know that cardinals love tiny cucumbers when they first come on. "Wings of Chance."

Now, getting back to Ben Dog, who became one of the greatest bird dogs I ever shot over. Ben was almost a constant companion around the house, in the garden, on the road and in the field. That companionship lasted for 15 years, until my wife, Bonnie, lost her bout with cancer. I had no one to care for Ben while I traveled, so I gave him to my hunting buddy and close friend, Jim Higgins. Jim at that time was deputy sheriff at Holden, Missouri. He had hunted over Ben many times and loved him as much as I did. Ben lasted a few more years. Jim gave him great care to the end!

I have written these things to prove that you can have a great hunting dog that is also a great house pet! Enough said.

The story doesn't end here, because Ben still lives on, on film. In 1953 an account executive at KCMO-TV, the CBS affiliate in Kansas City, Lee Martz, sold my TV show to the Ford Dealers of Kansas City. They bought the show for 13 weeks and kept it for 25 years. Lee and I worked together at KCMO-TV for about 15 years. He then went to a station in St. Joseph, Missouri, then to Davenport, Iowa, until he retired and moved back to Kansas City. The years wore on, and Lee's wife passed away. I saw him at her funeral, but never saw him again. In September of 2001 I received a telephone call from Lee. He said that he recently had an interesting experience that he wanted to share with me. He had just returned from Bozeman, Montana, where he visited an old friend. They had been doing something when his friend said, "It's time for my favorite TV program," and turned on the set. It was my show, which happened to be a re-run of a show we had made quail hunting with Ben Dog. I had done the re-run to honor Ben. Lee told him that he had sold that show in Kansas City in 1953. He said to Lee, "Do you really know that guy?" Lee told him that he had worked with me for many years. He then asked Lee if he had a chance to call me to see if he might be able to buy a dog from the same bloodline. I told Lee that I had no idea about finding the people who sold Ben to me. Lee and I had a nice visit on the telephone. Three weeks later Lee passed away in his sleep.

Yes, Ben Dog was a special dog to me, but he also had entertained people across the nation.

3

DURING 50 YEARS of broadcasting, I received many calls from farm groups and schools from Colorado, Kansas, Nebraska and Missouri to address their meetings. Almost always we would receive an invitation to hunt or fish in their area. We had a book full of names, addresses and telephone numbers. We were honored, but could never make it to all of them. However, we tried, and did make it to many of them.

I remember speaking to the Soil Conservation District in Medicine Lodge, Kansas. A man and his 12-year-old son came to me after the meeting. He said, "We have watched you hunt quail with Ol' Country Squire. We have lots of land and lots of birds; if you ever can come this way to hunt, we would be pleased to have you hunt on our place." He gave me his name and phone number. I put it in my billfold and forgot about it. Some ten years later, Larry North called me and said that he had arranged for a quail hunt near Medicine Lodge, Kansas. He had hunted with Bud Walton and me near Council Grove, Kansas. He wanted Bud and me to bring our dogs to hunt with him for three or four days. I called Bud. He was agreeable and said he had a new young pointer he wanted to try.

Medicine Lodge in south central Kansas is really off the beaten path. However, that area might just be the most scenic part of the state of Kansas. There is also a lot of frontier history from early days. I was delighted with the opportunity to hunt and shoot a quail movie there. The three of us drove down for the hunt. Larry was supposed to have a great place to hunt. It was good, but nothing like we expected!

The second night I happened to remember the farmer who had invited me years ago. I dug around in the notes and papers in my billfold. You won't believe it, but I found it! I called him and told him that we were in Medicine Lodge shooting a quail movie. I told him that we had just about finished our movie, but were about out of a place to hunt. I asked if the invitation to hunt his place for a day was still open. He was delighted to have us, but said his wife had some fancy chickens, and for us to watch our dogs. He gave us directions to his place and we drove out. He showed us the territory he wanted us to hunt. We had a good hunt and came back to our cars.

Bud said, "My legs are tired. I'm going to sit out the next round." He told us to take his young dog with us. I heard a racket and looked around; Bud's pup had caught one of the chickens. The old hen was squawking and feathers were flying. Then my young dog joined the fray. I yelled at Larry to grab a dog and help! I finally got the hen away from the dogs. She had lost a few feathers and was a little nervous. I had the boys hold the dogs while I carried the chicken to the barnyard and released it. She gave a couple of perks, shook herself and ran to the other chickens. I had that happen once before, years ago, and I think many other hunters have had a similar experience. Bud Walton was sitting in his pickup, laughing like crazy at what had happened. We put Bud's pup back in his pickup, and then made another run, finishing out our limit. We had four days of good weather and good hunting and made our movie.

The next morning we awakened to an ice storm. Bud headed for Bentonville and Larry and I for Kansas City. What do I remember about the trip? The beauty of the landscape, the good quail hunting, and finding a telephone number I had stashed away years ago, and that bird dog pup of Bud's pouncing on one of the lady's chickens. Many times it's the little things you remember most vividly.

For almost 50 years I carried a movie camera, catching the magic of the moment. I thought of the camera God had given us with our eyes. I thought of the memory bank of pictures recorded in our brains. How marvelous, that after all those years, in my mind I can pull up a picture of events of years gone by. I can close my eyes and pull up a picture of a rainbow that my son-in-law, Jim Trotter, and I saw above the Arctic Circle on Great Bear Lake. It was almost midnight, and the rainbow reached from one horizon to the other, and in the water a complete reflection. The rainbow on land touched the reflection in the lake. It was not a perfect circle, for the rainbow was not shaped in a perfect circle. Somewhere in our files, we have a still picture of it, but in my mind I can still pull up the picture, in color. I have no way of projecting it on a screen to others, but it's there on the screen of my brain. I can still pull up a scene of Country Squire on a point, then the sight of a covey of birds flushing. Every hunter or fisherman has his or her share of memories. There is a special bond between hunters and their dogs.

There is a saying that every hunter has a chance for one good bird dog in his lifetime. I called Audie Walton recently about Bud's favorite dog. She said that the dog's name was Jake. We had hunted many times, but I could not come up with the name of his special dog. I think Sam Walton's favorite dog was Ol' Roy, and the dog was made famous by Wal-Mart's Ol' Roy Dog Food. I remember one year, Sam called me and had some people he wanted to take on a big quail hunt. I arranged for a place near Manhattan, Kansas. Sam and his group were to fly into Manhattan. Dusty and I were to pick them up and take them to a ranch just south of the airport. The main thing I remember was that Sam had Ol' Roy and his other dogs. Ol' Roy was getting along in years. I made a special effort to get some movies of Sam and Ol' Roy. We had pretty well finished our picture and hunt when our host told us of another spot. We drove there and let the dogs out of the car.

Sam said, "Harold, why don't you get your gun and just leave the camera in the car?" I should have known better! We didn't get a half-mile until we came to a small shallow farm pond. It was frozen solid enough to walk on. There was a small patch of weeds and grass in the center of the pond. Ol' Roy ran out to that weed patch and made the most beautiful point he had made all day. The other dog honored his point. I said, "Sam, I'll go get my camera." He said, "No, it's probably just a rabbit!" We walked in and out flushed a covey of quail. I was sick! I missed a chance to get a shot of Ol' Roy on one of his most beautiful points. I can still see Ol" Roy standing proudly on that point. Memories are based on things like that.

Picture taken in Wal-Mart store at Lamar, Missouri, after hunting quail with Sam and Bud Walton, Jack Shewmaker and a local, whose name I cannot recall.

I remember another time when Jim Higgins, a deputy sheriff at Holden, Missouri, had invited Sam and me for a quail hunt near Clinton, Missouri. We drove to meet Sam at the airport at Clinton. We arrived about 15 minutes early, and Sam's plane was on the runway. A car was near, and in the cold the driver had the motor running. We asked him about Sam. He told us that the Wal-Mart store manager at Clinton had already picked up Sam and his dogs. He wanted us to meet him at the store. It was before the store opened for business, and Sam was having a meeting with his associates. When we came in, Sam called and said, "Ensley, grab a dog and I'll get a sack of dog food. You and I haven't had our picture taken together lately." The editor of the newspaper was there taking pictures. He was supposed to send me one, but didn't. It was misty rain and freezing, but we went hunting. Then Sam flew home. What do I remember about the hunt? It was Sam saying grab a dog and let's get a picture of us. Sam loved his dogs, as does every hunter!

Dusty, my younger son, is one of the best quail hunters I've ever hunted with. Dusty had a Brittany named Duke. We hunted with lots of hunters all over the Midwest. Duke would range with any pointer or setter and find as many birds. I would always prefer a stylish pointer or a setter for my movies because you could see them better in the picture. However, if I wanted a meat dog, I would welcome Duke anytime! We have heard it said that you couldn't have a good hunting dog and have it as a pet. That's not true!

In later years, I had a setter named Ben, that was the best dog I ever hunted over. We have already told you all about Ben. Speaking of dogs, we travel a lot and meet a lot

Dusty's Brittany on point.

of people. Three things they remember about my show: that I drove a red Ford Country sedan, that I had a bird dog named Country Squire, and my theme song, "Gone Fishin'." I've met people who remember that from 40-plus years ago.

We want to continue the thought of the little things that make you remember a hunting trip. A friend of mine, Don Brashears, called me and said that he had drawn a number for a goose-hunting pit at Swan Lake and wanted us to join him. He also invited our friend, Otto Oltmer.

Otto was not that much of a hunter, but really just went along for the ride. We really had to get up early to get to the state headquarters for a final draw for a particular pit. We arrived at the pit about 30 minutes before shooting time and settled in. Lots of geese were in the air. About five minutes before shooting time, some eight or ten big Honkers came directly over our blind, about 30 yards high. Don asked if we should take them. I said, "No way, it's still five minutes before shooting time!" We didn't shoot, and an hour later we hadn't seen another goose. Don said, "Maybe we should have shot that first bunch." It was a bluebird day, and lots of geese were moving, but up to that point none had come our way. Later in the morning, we had shot five geese and just lacked three for our limit. I said, "Boys, I'll take these geese in and have them cleaned and come back for you."

Then it dawned on me that I couldn't legally be carrying five geese at one time. So I asked Don to bring two geese and I would take two. We left Dusty and Otto in the blind and walked to my car. Two young men were standing there. One of them said, "Ensley, I need to see your license." Don and I showed them our licenses. He showed me his badge; he was a federal game warden. We visited awhile and he said, "Why didn't you shoot that first bunch?" I told him that it was before shooting time, but how did they know? He told me that they had been watching through their field glasses. As we drove in to take our geese, Don said, "Man, I'm glad we didn't shoot at that early flight." That's what I remember about that goose-hunting trip.

A man named Cal Banning called me from Warsaw, Missouri. He had just started developing an area on White Branch, just off the Osage River on the upper reaches of Lake Ozark just below Warsaw, Missouri. He was catering to outdoor people, both hunters and fishermen. He had been on my TV show and listened to my radio show. He wanted to know if he could become a reporter to my radio show for that area. I told him that all I asked was reliable reports. It worked out real well, as I had no one from that area reporting. We became friends and hunted and fished together many times. He and his wife, Mary, were friends to another couple out of Warsaw, Albert and Wanda Parker. Albert and his wife were dedicated quail hunters. Wanda, his wife, was a good shot, and my wife, Bonnie, became one of the best women quail shots I've seen. Mary wasn't much of a quail hunter, but the rest of us had a lot of good hunts together. Cal also had a lease for deer hunting and some duck blinds for rent. He invited Bonnie and me down to go duck hunting. Bonnie was not much of a duck hunter, for two reasons: she didn't like to get up early, and she had trouble hitting the ducks. We joined the two couples at White Branch and spent the night. We went out early the next morning. It was a beautiful day, but cold. Cal put the three women in a blind with me. He and Albert took the blind about 100 yards below us. Just at sunrise, the ducks started coming off Lake of the Ozarks, searching for feeding grounds.

Mary looked out and saw a big flock of mallards headed our way. She said, "Harold, why don't you start calling?" I said, "Mary, there's no way that I could break them up and get them in." To please her, I started calling. The ducks were high, but as long as I live, I'll never forget the sight as that lead drake cupped its wings and fell out of the sky. The rest of the bunch followed in spectacular fashion. Never in my life had I seen anything more beautiful! I made the girls stay down until the ducks were in range. I told them I wasn't going to shoot, so stand up and take them. Ducks were going around us in every direction. They emptied their guns and not a duck fell. Parker and Cal were in their blinds some 100 yards away and never had a duck close enough to shoot. I don't believe we saw another duck all day. I can close my eyes and see those 200 or 300 mallards set their wings to come into the decoys.

The next day we decided to try again. This time Parker and Cal had their wives in their blind, with us in the other blind. We had worked some small bunches into our decoys. I had shot a couple of mallards, but Bonnie kept missing. Finally she said, "When you see some ducks, you start calling and tell me to keep down in the blind. You tell me to keep my head down, and then say they are right over us; stand up and start shooting. I jump up and I have no idea where the ducks are. I start to shoot one and it falls. I swing to another and it falls. Next time, you stay down and do your calling. When the ducks are in range, you keep down and just let me shoot." I hadn't really thought about making it that difficult! After a bit, I saw five mallards working our way. I started calling. They made a swing to come in. When they were right over us, I told her the ducks would be right over in front, just pick out a duck and stay with it. She jumped up and started firing. She emptied her gun and not a duck fell. I was using my three-inch mag and decided to back her up. I shot and the duck fell. She said, "What do you mean killing my duck?" I said, "You missed it three times, could you call it your duck?" She said, "I'm sorry, I was just frustrated over missing the duck."

Bonnie didn't give up, but kept working until she became almost as good at duck hunting as she was at quail. A few weeks later, we were shooting a quail movie in central Kansas with a game warden friend of mine and his hunting buddy. We had a good hunt and finished the movie about mid-afternoon. I said, "Boys, we had a good hunt; Bonnie would like to shoot a few birds." They looked at one another as if to say we'll be here till dark. Bonnie fooled them. She shot eleven times and killed her limit of eight quail. I never had any more trouble with them when Bonnie was along. She loved to hunt and loved the bird dogs, especially Ol' Country Squire.

Speaking of love for dogs, perhaps no one loves their dogs more than the dog sled people of the north. One year at the Kansas City Sports Show, Nick Kahler brought a sled dog team from International Falls, Minnesota. A man named Schlessing owned the dogs, and they performed twice each day at the show. The dogs were beautiful, and it was a big thrill for us here in the Midwest to watch them perform. Their owner was a colorful person. During World War II he was hired to use his sled dog team on search and rescue missions on the DEW line for downed planes. Then, during the Battle of the Bulge, he and his dogs were flown to Europe to rescue wounded soldiers. He was a gracious man and loved his dogs.

I don't like the cold weather that much, although I shot ice-fishing in Michigan and Wisconsin. I had never been on snowshoes or followed a sled team through the snow. It seemed reasonable to join George at International Falls, Minnesota, to shoot a movie for our TV audience. I asked him about it and we arranged a trip. Dusty and I are both runners and thought we were prepared physically. When we met George at International Falls, the temperature was better than 30 degrees below zero. That was not wind chill, because in those days they didn't give wind chill. There was about 14 inches of snow on the ground. George had arranged for us to stay at a fishing camp on one of the lakes. He said that the weather was just right for our picture. We drove to the lake and drove out on the ice near where George had tethered the dogs in the snow near the shoreline. I couldn't believe that the dogs would be all right in the snow, but he fed them and said they would curl up in the snow and stay warm. He had a toboggan-like contraption behind his new snowmobile. He told us that we should just leave our car there and ride with him, about a mile across the lake. I looked at his outfit and decided to ride in the toboggan and let Dusty ride behind him on the snowmobile. That was a big mistake for me, as he took off at full speed across the lake. Little chips of ice came up in my face, and I don't think I ever caught my breath. Can you imagine what it was like in that toboggan behind the snowmobile at high speed? I told Dusty that in the morning he was going to be in the toboggan and I was going to ride in the snowmobile. The cabins were rustic, but comfortable.

George asked Dusty to get a bucket of water and handed him a spud and a bucket.

Dusty asked him where to get it. He told him out of the lake! Dusty was gone quite a spell, but came back with a bucket of water. He said, "That ice must be 12 inches through."

The next day the sun came out. We rode across to the car and the dogs. Man, was it cold, but we were dressed for it! George fed the dogs and took a shovel full of clean snow to each dog. I asked him what that was for. He said that was giving them a drink. They ate and lapped the new snow. George harnessed the dogs and put them in their place at the sled. He told us to put on our snowshoes and we would be ready. Dusty had filmed the whole procedure, and we took off through the woods. The setting

On snowshoes with George Schlessinger.

was beautiful, but it wasn't easy for me to keep up with the dogs on snowshoes. However, after three days of it, we began to become accustomed to it. We made our movie for TV, fished through the ice for walleye one day, and drove home. We were really impressed with George and his dogs. Those dogs were just like part of his family.

I believe that it was in the fall of 1970 I received a call from Enid, Oklahoma. They invited me to come down for the Grand National Quail Hunt, either as a reporter or as a contestant. I told them if I came down I would come as a contestant to try to win it, and we made arrangements for the date. I was to be in the new shooters division and to be on the Outdoor Writers team. At that time, I was shooting a 28-gauge Sportsman. It only held three shells. In the contest, you were allowed guns with five shells. I didn't think it was too smart to go up against shooters using a 12-gauge with five shells and me using a 28-gauge with only three. I borrowed a 12-gauge Remington 1100 from my friend, Ernie Simmons. They told me that each of the team shooters had to shoot 50 rounds of trap during the tournament. I could never afford to be a big-time trap shooter and didn't want to embarrass my teammates, so I went to my friend, Dean Edwards, who owned Midway Ford Truck Center, one of my TV sponsors. I told him my situation. I knew he was a dedicated trap shooter. He invited me to his gun club and let me use his trap gun to practice a few nights. After three or four nights, I was able to break 23 out of 25. He said, "Take my trap gun and you'll do all right."

I drove to Enid with no idea of what was to be there! There were several teams entered. Deke Slatton and the Astronauts had a team. There were other teams, which I don't remember. We had several days of quail shooting, then one day of skeet. I thought they were supposed to have one day of trap. Our outdoor team did well the first two days, and then one of our guys missed five birds. I was still in first place for the individual new shooters race. Fortunately, skeet shooting didn't play a part in the Championship Division, except for team honors. The other two members of our team asked me how I would do on skeet. I told them that I really never had shot skeet and they would have to show me where to stand. We were running neck-and-neck with the Astronauts for team honors. They said, "Ensley, you have carried us on the quail hunting; we will carry you on the skeet." We were to shoot 50 targets. They said that each of them would probably go straight, or at least be in the 48 or 49 class. That morning it was cold, and the wind was whipping across the Oklahoma prairie out of the north. The targets were dipping and darting. An army colonel from Maryland won the skeet shoot with 42 or 43. My two buddies each shot in the high 20s. I had a 39, which kept us in second place, behind Deke Slatton and his crew. I won a beautiful gold engraved Remington Model 11, 28-gauge shotgun for individual honors among the new shooters division. The Astronauts each won a like gun for winning the shoot. It was an honor to spend time with Deke and his crew. What a class act, the way they conducted themselves! We also shot with them in the Nebraska One-Box Pheasant Hunt at Broken Bow, Nebraska.

Sometime later, I received a letter from Slatton inviting my wife and me to Houston for their big game dinner. They had invited special friends from many parts of the world. Bonnie and I flew to Houston with our 12-year-old daughter for the event. We were there several days and were privileged to visit the Space Center. One night at dinner, Slatton asked me if my wife and I would like to go to Florida for the Apollo blast-off and sit in the VIP section. I said, "How would a peon like me get an invitation like that?" He said, "I don't know." Two weeks later we received a letter of invitation from the Space Administration Office. Bonnie and I drove to Florida and will always treasure the excitement of the moment.

The next year, Paul Weis and Rusty Swaggert flew up to Barksdale Air Force Base near Shreveport. We met them and fished several days at Toledo Bend and made a fishing movie. Every time I fished or hunted with them, I was always impressed with the way they conducted themselves. There is no question: they were among our bravest pioneers.

Speaking of pioneers, I received a call from the Daisy Company. They were marketing a new air rifle made in the likeness of a carbine. It was called the Buffalo Bill Edition. They said they had hired one of Buffalo Bill's descendants. He was either a grandson or great-grandson. They wanted him to be a guest on my TV show and present me with one of the air rifles. When I was a boy, Buffalo Bill was one of my heroes. I was pleased with the opportunity, and we arranged it. I was skeptical of his having any real connection with Buffalo Bill. He was a nice person, did a good job for Daisy and presented me with this Special Edition Air Rifle. After the show, we went to the switchboard to take my telephone calls. I had one call from an elderly lady at Sedalia. She asked if

Buffalo Bill's relative was still there. She said, "I taught him in school when he was a little boy." I asked here where she had taught him. She told me that it was in Cody, Wyoming. She was right, and he was the right one, and he remembered her and her name. They had quite a reunion on the phone, and it dispelled any thoughts I had about him being the real thing.

Occasionally, I have been asked why I hadn't taken up archery. There are several reasons; one being the condition of my right elbow. In the early years I had fished so hard that I ruined my right elbow. After undergoing surgery, I was informed that they had saved my arm, but it might be my last surgery, and to be very careful how I used it.

Archery certainly was not one of the activities that I needed. Archery hunting has been around for a long time, but no one ever dreamed to what extent bow hunting would go. Literally tens of thousands of hunters, both men and women, have taken up the sport. The great increase in the deer and turkey population has been responsible. It has been an explosion unlike anything else on the hunting scene.

In the late '60s my friend Rex Hancock at Stuttgart, Arkansas called me. He told me that they wanted me to judge in their world championship duck calling contest. They also told me that they were bringing in three nationally known archers and wanted me to shoot a movie of these three shooting ducks with a bow. Fred Bear, a legend in his own right, an archer from Arizona, and one from West Virginia. I cannot remember the names of the two, but Fred Bear was a class act! We stayed at Rex's home, and I had a chance to spend a lot of time with Fred. None of them killed a duck! Fred was good enough to kill a duck with a bow, if you could get the duck to hover over the decoys. However, with two or more archers standing by the blind, you could not get a duck close enough. We finally gave up and Fred hunted with me, with a gun. We had a good hunt and made a picture. He asked me if I would teach him to call ducks. I told him I would if he would come to Kansas City. It never worked out for either of us, but we later hunted together in Nebraska. We plan to use that later on in our book.

When I look back on the years, I think of how many opportunities for special trips with special people that I missed for lack of time. Thomas Hart Benton wanted to go to the Bridger Wilderness Area in Wyoming. Unfortunately, he passed away before we could do it. General Bowman wanted me to come back to Alaska to spend some time. He retired before we could make it! Doc of *Gunsmoke* called me and wanted to make another trip to God's Lake in Canada. We were scheduled to go to Africa for three weeks and couldn't make it. Doc passed away before we had another opportunity. You soon come to realize how fragile life is and that no one is going to be around forever.

Solomon, in the long ago, said, "Whatever your hand finds to do, verily do it with all your might; for there is no activity or planning or wisdom in Sheol where you are going" (Ecclesiastes 9:10). A good example of this was a case with Bobby Richardson, Yankee second baseman. The Yankees were in Kansas City for a series with the A's. I had taken Bobby and Tony Kubek fishing. I asked them if they would be guests on my TV show. They graciously obliged. During the show Bobby said, "Harold, you have been promising to come to South Carolina for a quail hunt. This fall I want you to come!" I told him I would!

After the show I was at the switchboard taking my phone calls. My friend, Ernie Simmons, was on the phone. He said, "If you go to South Carolina quail hunting, I'm going with you." I told him we would plan it. That winter we arranged it. I asked Bobby to get us a motel. He said, "No way, you two are going to stay with us." When I told Ernie about it, he said he wanted to stay at a motel. He said, "Bobby is such a nice guy, and real religious. He wouldn't want a character like me in his home." Nevertheless, when we flew to Columbia, Bobby met us at the airport and drove us to his home. We didn't take our dogs. Bobby had told us that a dog trainer would furnish the dogs and guide us. The first day Bobby's preacher wanted to go with us to watch us shoot the quail-hunting picture. I told Bobby it would be fine with me. So the preacher came with us, riding a Tennessee walking horse. He was a huge man! He must have weighed 300 pounds. He was proud of his horse and I suppose he thought he was at a field trial. When he saw a dog on point, he would yell, "Point Judge," and we would go to the dog and make a picture. Bobby's trainer was a good hunter and had good dogs. It was a mild winter day, just right for the hunt and for our movie. I was amused at the things he said to his dogs. If he wanted to change directions, he would say to the dogs, "All right, you dogs, I'm gone." He would then change directions and the dogs would follow. If one dog was on a point, he would yell at the other dog, "All right, Sam, you see that dog," and Sam would freeze to honor the other dogs point. We were hunting reforested timberland. The young trees were about six or eight feet high with lots of sage grass. It made ideal cover for the birds and for shooting conditions. Bobby is an excellent shooter and, of course, Simmons was. We found lots of quail, and when we finished the movie, I got a chance to hunt.

It was unseasonably warm and late in the afternoon; the preacher was still on his horse. He had a canteen on his saddle. He said to Ernie, "Mr. Simmons, do you want a drink?" Ernie told him that he did. The preacher handed the canteen to him. He took a big swig and then spit water all over. He said, "Preacher, that's water! I thought you asked me if I wanted a drink." It was funny, but you had to know Ernie Simmons to appreciate it. We had a good time with Bobby and his family. I didn't see him until several years later.

Dusty and I were working a Western Auto Dealer show in Charlotte, North Carolina. At that time, Western Auto was one of my major sponsors. In the meantime, Bobby had retired from the Yankees and was coaching the South Carolina University baseball team. I called Bobby and he drove to Charlotte to see us. I told him it had been a long time since I had played baseball, but I would like to work out with his team. We drove down, spent the night, and the next day went over to workout with his boys. I told him I wanted to have Dusty take a movie of him pitching to me in batting practice. Old dumb me; I picked out a wooden bat instead of an aluminum one. Dusty was taking pictures. He said, "Dad, you are swinging after the ball has gone past." After about 20 minutes, I got to pulling the ball okay. I didn't show my television audience how bad I did at first. Dusty picked up an aluminum bat and rattled the fence with ease, as did Bobby. We didn't see Bobby after that, but have been in contact with him. I was visiting with him on the phone recently. We talked about our quail hunting days. We had started him and several of the Yankee players into shooting 28-gauge guns. He told me that he is now shooting a 28 over and under, as does Dusty. He said, "Harold, it's not like it used to be here. We just don't have any wild birds anymore."

He then told me that he bought 100 birds and put them out for his family. Unfortunately, that has happened in many areas. The good old quail hunting days have disappeared in many places. My friend Buddy Baier was way ahead of his time when he started a commercial shooting ground for quail, pheasant and chukar partridge. Buddy started his place near Peculiar, Missouri back, in 1952 or 1953 and is still doing business today. Business executives from as far away as Chicago and Minneapolis still fly here to hunt his place. What we lost in quail, we gained in wild turkeys and deer. We probably have more wild turkey and deer than the early pioneers found here. Countless thousands of men and women have been addicted to hunting wild turkey. It is really an addiction! The Southern states have been blessed with lots of wild turkeys for years.

I remember Enos Slaughter 40 years ago telling me about hunting wild turkey in Texas. He would shoot a turkey and cut out the big part of the wing bone to make a turkey call. By the way, I talked to Enos by telephone in Roxboro, North Carolina. He was the same old Enos and had been hunting deer that day.

Years and years ago the people of the little town of Yellville, Arkansas held what they called the National Wild Turkey Calling contest. For several years I was called to be their Master of Ceremonies. It would be quite an event for their city. I don't know when they started it or if they still do it. They would toss live tame turkeys with money tied around their necks out of low-flying airplanes. The crowd would chase the birds down. If you caught a turkey, you got to keep it and the money. It didn't hurt the birds, and crowds gathered to try their luck. There were few turkey calls on the market and very few turkey callers. Today, the turkey call business is big time and thousands have become effective callers. My son Dusty is an avid caller and hunter. I was never bitten by the turkey-calling bug. However, I killed my first wild turkey in Texas.

My friend, Ernie Simmons, called and told me he had been invited to Texas for a wild turkey hunt and would like for me to go with him. He said, "You took me to South Carolina for quail hunt; now I want you to go to Texas with me." He told me that a friend of his, a famous pistol shooter, Col. Askins, wanted us to fly down to Fort Sam Houston and stay at his place. We flew down. The Colonel met us at the airport and took us to his home. I was hardly prepared for the elegance of his house, and I don't think Ernie was either. We were just two country bumpkins. I was going to try to make a movie for my show, but it didn't work out that way. The Colonel told us that due to some unforeseen changes in his schedule, he could not hunt with us. He had made arrangements for a sergeant to take us to the hunting spot on the base. It was a nice day and I was really excited about shooting my first wild turkey. They took us to a tree stand. They had built a platform about ten feet square and about eight feet above the ground between two trees. They had steps built to reach the platform. They left us, telling us that they would come get us later in the day. I had my movie camera and my shotgun. We hadn't been on the stand long before about ten birds came into sight, five of them were gobblers. The air was dead calm, and when I started the movie camera, it spooked them and they took off.

Neither Ernie nor I could call, so we had to wait and hope some more would come within range. We were comfortable on the platform and soon saw five more turkeys working our way. Ernie whispered for me to forget my camera and get my gun. There were three Toms and two hens. One of the Toms was huge, but he was on my side. Ernie said, "I know it doesn't make any difference to you, but I want to shoot that big Tom." I really didn't mind, but we were actually shooting across each other. We fired a couple of shots and never got a bird. I said, "Ernie, if we have a next time, you shoot the birds on your side." We were beginning to think we had really messed up! We saw four more birds coming. All Toms! When the birds came within range, Ernie whispered, "Let's take them!" We each fired twice and all four birds fell. I heard a grunt. I looked around for Ernie. He was so excited he just stepped off the platform. When he hit the ground the gun went one way and Ernie the other. I asked him if he was all right. He said, "Yes, but watch that first step, it's a long one." I couldn't believe he dropped that far without injury!

We went out to pick up the turkeys and two of them had revived and taken off. He came back and said, "We still may have time to get our other two birds." Back then, we were allowed two birds each. However, they came to pick us up before we had another chance. They took them to a locker plant, removed the entrails and froze the birds. The next day we were to fly home. We each had a frozen turkey in a bag, with its head showing. It caused no small stir when we climbed aboard with a wild turkey in our arms. However, you have to know Ernie Simmons to understand that there was never a dull moment with him! He and I had a lot of great hunting trips after that, but I can still see the look on his face when he picked up his gun after stepping off that platform!

Wild turkey hunting is commonplace now in this part of the country, and the birds are plentiful. When I think of our forefathers, the brave pioneers that founded our country, I doubt they would have made it without wild game. Occasionally, we find people who complain about killing and eating wild game. God gave us these things for food. When Noah and his family stepped out of the ark on dry ground, God said, "Be fruitful and multiply and fill the earth. And the fear of you and the terror of you shall be on every beast of the earth and every bird of the sky with everything that creeps on the ground and all the fish of the sea into your hand they are given. Every moving thing that is alive shall be food for you. I give all as I gave the green plant. Only you shall not eat flesh with its life, that is its blood" (Genesis 9:1-4). However, not much is said in the scripture about hunters. Nimrod was said to be a great hunter. It was said of Ishmael that he became an archer. We learn the patriarch loved wild game (Genesis 27:2-3).

Issac said to Esau, his son, "Behold now I am old, and do not know the day of my death. Now then please take your quiver and bow and go out into the field and hunt game for me. And prepare a savory dish as I love and bring it to me that I may eat so that my soul may bless you before I die." Verse 5 said that Esau went to the field to hunt for game to bring home. Certainly God gave these things to eat and to enjoy.

4

YEARS AGO I was hunting with a retired army sergeant in central Kansas. He invited me to hunt quail with him and General Seitz at Fort Riley, Kansas. We arranged a date. I told him I would need to cover the hunt for my TV show. We drove to Junction City to meet the general. The sergeant had a pointer, and I had Country Squire and a pretty little white female English setter called Susie. Susie was not much of a bird dog, but was a beautiful addition in the field with Country Squire. Susie never found many quail, but looked good in the movies honoring Squire's points. Susie also looked good retrieving the birds she found. We were to hunt on the reservation at Fort Riley. I had heard reports of the great numbers of quail on the base.

It's strange that it might be one small incident which makes you remember a hunt. General Seitz had watched my TV shows and was elated about hunting over Country Squire. The weather was beautiful, with bright sunshine. It was just the kind of day for movie-making. However, we didn't find many quail or pheasant. We had hunted a couple of hours when the sergeant called from the other side of the fence row. He said that Squire and his dogs were on a point, and for us to come over. The general and I started to go when we noticed Susie was on a solid point near a small patch of grass. It was just right for a picture, with bright sunshine and out in the open. It wasn't a likely looking spot, and I thought it might be a false point. Nonetheless, I told the sergeant to stand over Squire and his dog, that Susie was on point and that we were going to get some pictures of her. I took the preliminary shots and asked General Seitz to kick up the bird. He did, and to our surprise a rooster pheasant roared into the air. The bird was so close, and taken by surprise he missed the bird the first two shots. The third shot killed the bird. Little Susie ran out and retrieved the bird. It was a beautiful sight, the white setter with that brilliantly colored pheasant in her mouth. One wing was over one side of her head. I shot pictures of the retrieve and the general taking the bird from Susie's mouth. He turned to me and I saw he had tears in his eyes, being so moved by the moment. I don't remember much more of the hunt, although we did find a lot more quail. "Wings of Chance."

The next time I worked with General Seitz, he called me to be at the dedication of the Corps of Engineers Project at Wilson Dam and Reservoir. He was a great guy and became a good friend. I received an invitation to hunt near Fort Leavenworth, Kansas, with General Hay. He had commanded Big Red over in Viet Nam. He was a friend of one of my friends and wanted to hunt with us. We arranged the trip and met at Fort Leavenworth. We were to hunt on a farm south of there. The General had a young Brittany spaniel and asked if he could take the dog with us. We were having a good hunt, but the

Pheasant hunting in western Kansas with my son-in-law, Dr. Jim Trotter, and Blair Flynn.

Brittany had not lived up to the General's expectations. About midday someone crippled a quail. It could barely fly, but managed to make it over the hill out of our sight. The General's Brittany chased the bird, and it also went out of sight. I asked the General if the Brittany would bring the bird back if he caught up with it. He was pretty disgusted with his dog and promptly said no! We looked up, and over the hill came his Brittany, with the bird in its mouth. The Brittany brought the bird to the General. I don't know if the dog was more proud of getting the bird, or if the General was more proud of his dog. We had a good hunt and the General was a great guy, but I never saw him after that. "Wings of Chance."

One year Dusty and I were called to some kind of special hunt for pheasant. I don't recall whether it was Minnesota or South Dakota. We were pleased when told that we were to hunt with Harmon Killibrew. I had watched Harmon hit home runs for the Minnesota Twins many times, but had never met him personally. Dusty, Harmon and I made one run that day and each had killed a few pheasant. After one drive, we went back to my station wagon to get a drink of water and leave what pheasant we had shot. It was a warm day, and a few pheasant in your coat, plus your shotgun shells, got heavy. Harmon had put a couple of roosters in the front seat. We were making a movie as we hunted. As the afternoon wore on, we finished out our limit of birds and came back to the wagon. I approached the wagon from the driver's side, and Harmon came in from the opposite side. I looked in the car and could see a live rooster pheasant walking around in the front seat. It had apparently revived! I could hear Harmon unloading his shotgun. I could just visualize what was going to happen when he opened the car door. I motioned for Dusty to get the camera ready to capture the moment. It didn't happen that way. Harmon saw the live bird and didn't open the car door until we were in a position to catch the bird. Harmon corralled the bird and spoiled our fun. With a sheepish grin he said, "I have to watch you guys and your tricks, even back at the car."

Harmon was a great one, and it was an honor to hunt with him. We never hunted with him again. The last time I heard from him he was selling real estate in Idaho. He had a listing from a hunting and fishing lodge in Idaho and thought I might know of someone who might be interested in buying it. I later shot a salmon fishing movie on the middle fork of the Salmon River. However, I did not have a chance to call him. What do I remember about our hunting trip? It wasn't the pheasants we bagged, but that old rooster that had revived and was walking around in the station wagon. Much to my surprise, as I was working on this book, I received a call from him and he was in Kansas City signing autographs. Our schedules didn't allow us to meet, but it was wonderful to hear from him. I asked if he remembered that rooster walking around in my station wagon. He laughed and said, "You and Dusty will never forget that!"

Dusty and I were hunting quail with Tom Watson in Central Kansas one day. We were having a good hunt and found lots of quail. Dusty brought Duke, his Brittany. Duke was as fine a bird dog as you could find anywhere. We came to a patch of knee-high grass. The pointers were off to the side in some timber. Duke came down on a solid point. Dusty got the camera ready and we asked Tom to walk in, flush the bird and kill it. Tom walked up by Duke's side and started to kick the bird out. It was a skunk! Duke grabbed the skunk and started shaking it. Watson took off in one direction and Dusty the other. I was yelling at Dusty to get a picture. Duke was trying to bring the skunk to either Tom or Dusty. We had a good hunt and finished our picture. Dusty had to ride home with a dog that smelled like skunk. "Wings of Chance."

When I was a boy in western Kansas, I started hunting sharks' teeth in the many eroded areas of our ranch. I really don't remember my first time, but it had to be at a tender age. The ironic thing is that I don't know who started me at it, or how I came to know them as sharks' teeth. I don't remember my dad ever doing it. I have no idea when that part of the world was under water, but at least I believe, sincerely, that God once flooded the whole world in Noah's time. Most of the sharks' teeth and fossils we found in the yellow shale of the eroded areas, and also some in the Chalk Bluffs of western Kansas. My brother and I almost knew them by heart. If we weren't doing our chores, working in the field or hunting or fishing, we were hunting for sharks' teeth. After I had been on television a few years, I was in my hometown of Healy, Kansas, to visit my sister and her family. I had a day free to roam around the old home place. It has long been deserted, and the old building is gone. I always took my movie cameras with me just in case I

Hunting sharks' teeth in western Kansas.

stumbled onto extra program material. I was by myself and decided I would take pictures of the creek where I did my first fishing. It was winter, and though the sun was out, it was cold. The creek was frozen solid, and it didn't inspire me. I drove to an eroded area on the northwest part of the ranch. I decided to try to find some sharks' teeth. It took me almost an hour to get my eyes adjusted. I found one, then found another. Then the idea hit me. Why not show one of the eroded areas and looking for sharks' teeth on my TV show? I drove into town, got my brother-in-law, Ellsworth Stewart. We drove back to the ranch. I showed him how to run the movie camera. He took pictures of me looking for sharks' teeth and finding them. The next day I drove back to Kansas City and had the film processed to be ready for my show. Then I got to thinking that I had better check before I went on the air saying these are sharks' teeth when maybe they are not. So I went to the library and found a magazine which contained an article on sharks. Sure enough, the teeth that I picked up in western Kansas were identical to the ones shown in the modern magazine. I ran the film on my show, and the response was wild. Science teachers and people from almost every walk of life called. Even to this day I get calls from people wanting to know where to go to find them. Just recently, some 45 years later, I had a man ask me about it. Fort Hays Teachers College has a museum with many kinds of fossils from the Chalk Cliffs and shale eroded areas of western Kansas.

About 30 years ago I drove to Bentonville, Arkansas, to call on the Wal-Mart stores.

A friend of mine learned that I was going. They called and asked me if I would drive over near Rogers, Arkansas, to buy them some elderberry jelly. They had heard of a small gift shop on Highway 71 near Rogers that also sold jams and jellies. I finally located the store. I went in to see if they had any elderberry jelly for sale. While they were getting the jelly, I looked at a picture hanging on the wall. I could hardly believe my eyes. It was a picture of a fossilized fish that had just swallowed another smaller fish. I knew of no picture like that except one; it had to be of the fossil in Professor Steinberg's Museum in Hays, Kansas. I asked the proprietor where in the world he came up with that picture. I told him that I grew up not far from where the fossil was found. Then he told me the story. He had been born in Russell Springs, Kansas. While he was just a boy, walking down a dirt road to school one day he saw a brown paper bag in the road ditch. Out of curiosity, he picked it up and took it to his mother. They found two rolls of film, and there was an address on the boxes. It belonged to Professor Sternberg in Hays, Kansas. It was a roll of film that contained the shot of the fossil of one fish that had swallowed the other. His mother mailed the film to Professor Sternberg, who, in appreciation, sent his mother an enlarged picture. I assumed that his mother had passed on and had given it to him. I could hardly believe that he had it, and he could hardly believe that I knew of it! Yes, the "Wings of Chance" blow from many directions. In case you don't believe that the big fish swallowed the small one, stop in at Sternberg's Museum in Hays, Kansas and see for yourself. If you ever want to hunt for sharks' teeth and fossils, they can be found in the eroded canyons where you find white or yellow shale. Drive Highway I-70 to western Kansas. We have done the best in the eroded ravines along the Smokey Hill River, on both sides of the valley, from Quinter, Kansas, almost to the Colorado line. The region just north of Scott City and south of Oakley, Kansas is an excellent area, also.

Hell's Bar, an eroded area in northeast Scott County, Kansas. A typical area to hunt sharks' teeth.

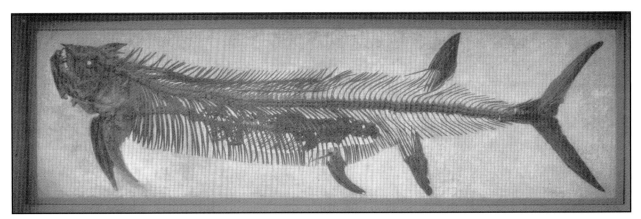

Fossil found in western Kansas — fish swallowed smaller fish. Now in Sternberg Museum at Fort Hays, Kansas.

I cannot recall the exact date, but it must have been at least 30 years ago, we received a call from a conservationist at Silver Creek, Nebraska. He had planned a special conservation week for their area and had invited so-called celebrities from across the nation. The special guests were to work on wildlife habitat and feeding areas. They invited us to come to help promote the project. They said that they wanted us to take movies for my TV show and to do some hunting. We were always looking for material for our weekly TV show. We were also always interested in any effort that was being put forth to promote wildlife conservation. I was thrilled to learn that Dusty and I had been paired with Roy Rogers and the famous archer, Fred Bear. Both of them were legends in their own fields. We considered it a great honor. I had worked with Fred Bear hunting ducks at Stuttgart, Arkansas, but we had never been with Roy Rogers. Can you imagine building brush piles for wildlife cover and other projects with Roy Rogers and Fred Bear? Can you imagine hunting squirrels and rabbits with them? We did, and also hunted ducks and pheasant! Roy, Fred, Dusty and I all stayed together in one house, giving us an opportunity to visit together. One morning before daylight, they took Roy and me to a duck blind on an island in the Platte River. We were given chest-waders and had to wade in a treacherous current, with quicksand around. We loaded our decoys and guns in an aluminum Jon boat, but we had to wade. We had two local guides who pulled the boat. Roy was wading on one side of the boat, and I was on the other. We were each holding on to the boat as we waded. We made it to the island without mishap, but at one point the current swept me off my feet. It was a scary moment. Being in the cold waters of the Platte is no place to be with chest-waders. Should you lose your hold on the boat in the darkness, it would all be over quickly! However, it was a perfect place to hunt ducks. They had a good blind on the island. It was just about daylight when the guides put out the decoys. I really don't remember whether we shot any ducks, but sometime that morning I heard a white-front goose calling. It was a single goose, coming in high and a few hundred yards out. I asked Roy if he had ever killed a white-front goose. He said, "I've never seen one!" I started calling. I told Roy here was his chance to kill one. The goose made a pass over the duck decoys, and Roy dropped it. He was a good hunter.

Duck hunting with Roy Rogers in Silver Creek, Nebraska.

We later went with Fred and Dusty pheasant hunting. Dusty said he thought they brought Fred in to shoot a pheasant with a bow. I really don't remember that, but I do know that Fred Bear was capable of hitting a pheasant in the air, if he had the right situation. Then one afternoon the four of us went squirrel and rabbit hunting with our .22 rifles. It was the first time I had hunted squirrel in many years, and I'm sure that Fred and Roy hadn't hunted them in years, either. We had a great time! It was a big moment for Dusty and me, but we never had another opportunity to spend time with them.

Speaking of hunting squirrels, that may have been my last time. It's strange that the number of deer and turkey hunters has increased in explosive proportions, but I hardly ever hear of many squirrel or rabbit hunters. I mentioned early in this book about the importance of wild game to our forefathers, and squirrels and rabbits were a part of it. I like to eat both rabbit and squirrel. I don't mind cleaning rabbits, but squirrels are a little more trouble. When God gave us wild game and fish, he gave us wonderful food. Cleaning and taking proper care of it is important. In our 48 years of doing our TV show, we had many viewers call us about dressing and preparing wild game. We were constantly looking for program material. The "Wings of Chance" flew our way with just those opportunities.

Some 40 years ago a viewer called suggesting I use a friend of his on my show to pick ducks. He told me that he had hunted in a duck blind many times. He said that this guy would pick and dress the ducks as they shot them. When they were ready to drive home, the ducks were ready for the pan. He gave me his name and telephone number, and I called him. He was reluctant to do it, but finally consented. However, the ducks had to be fresh-killed and still warm. There was no way we could work that to get wild ducks, so we bought a couple of tame ducks for the demonstration. I was told that he could pick a duck and have it ready for the pan in either three or five minutes. It's been so long ago, my memory bank couldn't bring it up for me, exactly. I can't remember either of the names. This was live television, and we didn't have enough ducks for a rehearsal. We started the show. The man was absolutely amazing and did exactly what he said he could do. That wasn't the whole 30 minutes of the show, but he certainly entertained our TV audience. I think everyone who watched wanted to take him hunting. Some few years later, I started to get mail requesting a return performance. He was an older man, and a busy man. Although I don't remember his name, I do remember that he was the head of a big transportation company here in the Midwest. I called to ask him to repeat his performance, that I had received a large number of requests to have him back. He politely refused. I kept insisting. He was a rough talker. He finally said, "I'll do it, but you're the only s.o.b. that I would do it for!" We arranged the date. Again, he did an excellent job. The switchboard lit up with calls. I remember one lady who called from Humansville, Missouri, a little town north of Springfield. She wanted to challenge him to a contest. That, again, was the fun of live television.

I received a call from a chef at Eddy's Famous Restaurant in Kansas City. I don't recall his last name, but his first name is Leon. He wanted to come on my show and prepare wild game. I welcomed his suggestion, and we made the arrangements. He wanted to cook moose, elk, deer, bear, quail and pheasant. He told me that he had friends who would furnish everything but the quail and pheasant. It turned out to be an exciting show, and fun. My crew loved it because they became the taste-testers. Chef Leon had just the right French flair to make it entertaining. I had been cleaning quail for years, but he taught me something that I use to this day. I want my quail fried and had never figured out a way to fry it properly, because of its shape. Chef Leon severed the legs, pulled the neck and back out and threw it away, then split the breast so it would be flat. It worked beautifully! Then dip the legs and split breasts in buttermilk, roll them in flour, and either deep-fry or pan-fry them. To me, God didn't make anything better than that! However, if you don't split the breasts and fry them, you have to cook the outside too long to get the inside done. If you prefer to bake them whole, you can, but try Chef Leon's way, at least one time. I made myself hungry just writing about it. Chef Leon's duck, goose, deer and antelope were also very good, but I could have done without the bear!

Speaking of food, God didn't make anything better than fresh strawberries, fully ripened, out of your own garden, or a fully ripened tomato, picked off the vine. I love the soil and I love to garden. The miracle of all miracles is to plant a seed and watch it grow to maturity and bear fruit. At a tender age, I helped my mother plant garden on our ranch in western Kansas. That is dry country and usually you had to put water in the row before you planted the seed.

Many families in today's world could help themselves by raising a garden. People give all kinds of excuses: I don't have time, I don't have a big place, and besides, it's a chore. However, some people do not "like" to hunt, fish, jog or garden. That's why God gave us choices. Gardening for me is not a chore, it's a pleasure.

Several times I was invited to hunt bear in Alaska and Canada, but I had no desire to eat a bear. Therefore, I had no desire to kill one. However, I have several bear stories, but will share only three with you. One from Canada's Northwest Territory, one from God's Lake in Manitoba, and one from Churchill, in Manitoba.

The first one I will tell you about took place within the city limits of Churchill. It was the second consecutive summer that our friend Barney Lamm asked Dusty and me to guide his fishing party at Chantry Inlet. Dusty and I drove to Fort Francis, Ontario, where Barney's pilot met us and flew us to Barney's Ball Lake Lodge, just east of Kenora, Ontario. There we met the ten fishermen from Dallas that we were to guide. We were to fly in a P.B.Y. to Churchill, refuel there, then fly on to Chantry Inlet at the edge of the Arctic Ocean. Rex Kitely, a veteran bush pilot, and his co-pilot, whose name I do not recall, were to fly us there. In our first book, *Winds of Chance,* we wrote of our first trip. It was wild and rugged country, but the terrain at Chantry was really not as bad as that where the Tree River runs into the Arctic Ocean. We, of course, were above the timberline, not a tree or a bush anywhere, just bare rugged hills. Baker Lake was the nearest source of fuel. It was some 600 miles from Chantry. There was no camp there, and no firewood. A small band of Eskimos camped there to catch their fish for the winter months. It is the most barren fishing spot we ever found, but plenty of mosquitoes, and fabulous lake trout fishing. Our first and only stop was Churchill, to refuel.

While they were refueling, we rented taxis to go into town to have lunch. Dusty and I had the same taxi driver that we had the year before. That year we were forced by weather to spend an afternoon and night in Churchill. The taxi driver remembered us from the previous trip and knew that we were taking movies for our TV show. Before we left the airport, he suggested that I take my camera. He told us that there was a wild polar bear right downtown and we might get some pictures. It was not uncommon for this to happen in Churchill. They had tried to chase the bear back into the wild, or to capture it and take it back a ways and release it unharmed. The bear became frightened and took refuge under a huge lumber warehouse. The warehouse was built on large pilings to keep it above the water line in case of high water. The floor of the building was some six or eight feet above the ground, making an ideal place for the bear to hide. They had tried to entice the bear out with a fish, and the man holding the fish was mauled by the bear and was taken to a hospital. At least that was the story they gave us.

A Canadian Royal Mounted Policeman with a rifle was guarding the place. They had roped off an area to keep people from getting too close to the building. The taxi driver took us to the spot and agreed to stand by. The Mounty would not let us get close enough to take pictures, so the taxi driver took us to the café where the rest of the group was having lunch. Dusty and I ordered a bite to eat. The taxi driver came running in and told us that the mounty had gone to lunch. He was sure we could get some pictures. Dusty wanted to go, but I told him to eat his lunch, that I could handle it, but to get me a sandwich because we were running out of time. The taxi driver took me to the lumber storage area, but on the opposite side from where we had been the first time. The police had roped off an area covering several acres of ground to keep the crowd back out of danger. There were possibly 200 people gathered back of the roped off section. From there, you could see the bear under the building. It appeared to be dead, so I asked some bystanders if the bear had been shot. Some teenage boys said, "Yes, Mister, they shot it."

I walked through the mud for nearly 100 yards. I took some pictures of the building with the mounty's rifle leaned up against the door. The bear was motionless, and I really thought it was dead. I walked close enough that the bear's head filled the screen of the camera. I had been close to big bears and shot pictures of them at Katmai National Park in Alaska. This Polar bear was huge, but I could not get a picture of the entire body. I was so engrossed in getting pictures that I didn't notice an Indian with his dog coming down the railway tracks at the edge of the building.

When the bear heard the dog bark and stood up, it gave a growl that was almost blood-chilling, and charged out! I started to run and slipped and fell. I was crawling on my hands and knees in the mud. When the bear hit the bright sunlight, it was evidently blinded, and it stopped in its tracks! I finally got on my feet and ran the rest of the way.

The crowd thought it was funny, especially the teenagers who told me the bear was dead. I don't know what happened to the Indian and his dog, and never did hear what happened to the bear. The rest of the trip to Chantry Inlet was uneventful. We caught lots of Trophy Lake trout and everyone was happy. 'Nuff said!

Bear stories two and three are especially for my jogging friends. Every time I made a trip to Alaska and had an opportunity to jog, I was very much aware of the possibility of coming upon a bear. In fact, near Katmai Lodge, I asked Tony Saarp if there was a trail where I could run. He warned me of the possibility of seeing a bear. I never had any problem there, but Tony flew us to the Katmai National Park, where there were almost as many bears as people. We had several skirmishes there, but if you listened to the park people, you had no problem. It's a beautiful park and should be a must for anyone touring Alaska. In Canada's Northern Territory on Great Bear Lake, Warren Plummer moved his lodge from the south side of the lake to the Dease Arm, which is just above the Arctic Circle. It was quite a project to move the buildings across the lake. Of course, they had to do it in the dead of winter when the ice was thick. They built the lodge on an island, but built an airstrip on the mainland across the bay. The first time we went there we flew in a DC3 from Yellow Knife. He later expanded the strip to accommodate a DC6, then in later years, 737 jets. It was a dirt strip, and if I remember correctly, a little over 5,000 feet long. You would land on the strip and walk about 300 yards to the water's edge. The guides would meet us in boats and take us to the lodge.

A few years later, they built a dirt road from the lodge, around the bay to the airstrip, and brought in a school bus to transport fishermen from the airstrip to the lodge. I estimated the distance from the lodge to the far end of the runway to be close to three miles. That made a round trip by this trail at least six miles. The first few years, it was a pretty rough to jog on the rocky spots. Each year, it was made a little better. I could get up early and run, or wait until we came in. We were supposed to have our guides in by 6 p.m. That gave me time for a good run before dinner. To me, it was a beautiful place to run, as the trail followed a ridge around the perimeter of the bay. We usually made the trip in late July. The days were still long and there were lots of Arctic flowers in places where it had been graded. From the trail, almost all the way, you could look down on the water. It was always a special time for me.

One evening, I was daydreaming as I ran, and I thought how wonderful that God had made a place like this and had given me the privilege of being there. The trail went past their garbage dump about a mile from the lodge. Occasionally, a grizzly bear would be seen there. As I came near the spot, for some reason I thought of bears. I had just completed five miles of my run. I knew I couldn't outrun a bear if I were fresh, much less make it when I was tired. I had just rounded the bend in the trail and started past the garbage dump. Something hit me in the back with a sound that would chill your blood. A raven had hit me and let out a squawk like I'd never heard before. I suppose it had a nest nearby and thought I was intruding. It would have shocked me more if it had been a bear, but had it been a grizzly, I wouldn't be here to tell about it.

My third and last bear story comes from God's Lake in Manitoba. A young attorney

A special tribute to Judge Sal Nigro, my duck-hunting buddy, and his son Billy. This is the only photograph I have of him. THOSE were the days, when we kept our fish.

in Kansas City, Sal Nigro, did all my contract work with endorsements. He loved to fish and hunt. He became one of my best friends, and we fished and hunted together many times. In later years, he became a municipal judge, but still managed to find time to make a few trips with us. One year, he wanted to take his son Billy. We arranged a date on God's Lake to fish at Barney Lamm's East Bay Camp, and invited our friend Maurice O'Link of St. Cloud, Minnesota to join us. Sal, Maurice, and I made many trips together, but it was Billy's first time that far north. It is an exciting moment when your dad takes you fishing, and Billy was making the most of it. We had beautiful weather and caught lots of fish. We also made a movie for our TV show. Really, it was combining work with pleasure. The days were long, and each evening after dinner Billy and I would get our jogging done. I never worried about bears around God's Lake. Occasionally, you would see one, but the natives kept them on the move. As far as I know, there were only black bears in that area. So it was not like being in Grizzly or Kodiak country. The walls of the dining room at Barney's East Bay Lodge were graced with mounted trophy fish, a trophy moose head, a trophy buck deer, and by the fireplace, a mounted black bear. It was mounted in a standing position with its front legs and claws as though in an attack position. This particular evening, Billy and I had almost completed our run. We used a narrow trail back of the lodge. It was not the best place to run, with the tree roots and rocks; however, it was adequate for our purpose. The trail was so narrow we had to run single file. I was leading the way with Billy on my heels. The sun had gone down, but the twilight hours in the far north make a very pleasant time to run. Just before you reach the lodge, the trail makes a sharp bend around a tree. Again, I was daydreaming as I ran; just as I came around the tree, I ran right into the arms of a bear, with Billy right on top of me. Some pranksters had carried the mounted bear out of the lodge and set it on the trail as it made the bend around the tree. I didn't have a heart attack, but I got a good scare. Everybody at the lodge was waiting for the moment and thought it was funny. Billy and I didn't see it that way at the time. We had a great trip. Sal has since passed away, but Billy and I are still close friends. I saw him recently, and we laughed about the bear incident. Billy said, "I caught more fish that trip than I had caught anywhere. One of my fondest memories is fishing with Dad and you." Really, that's what it's all about, so to you dads, I say take your sons or daughters fishing. To the sons and daughters, take your dad and mom on a trip. You'll be glad you did!

Just recently, we went to a supermarket to get groceries. It so happens that they have a delicatessen and small café area where you can order and eat. It was lunch and most of the tables were occupied. Four young men were seated at a table near the door. As I walked by them, one man asked me what my name was. I told him, and he said, "I have watched your TV shows since I was a little boy." One of the other men said, "Harold, you took me fishing when I was just a boy." I asked him where and when. He told me that when he was a Boy Scout, I fished with their scout troop for trout on the White River in Arkansas. I said, "Yes, we did. We put in at Cotter, Arkansas, and camped on an island a few miles down stream and fished in the river near the island." They didn't feel that they could afford guides, but had several dads who fished and would handle the boats. They had planned to float and fish the river for three days and take out at Buffalo Shoals. I said, "Since you dads have never handled a boat in that kind of water, I don't think you should try it that distance. It could be difficult for you if they start generating power at the dam." The water pours through the turbines and the river becomes a raging current. When the turbines are running, it's just not safe for a bunch of scouts and three dads!

I suggested that they float from Cotter to an island and camp there. Under no circumstances did I want them going over Buffalo Shoals without veteran guides. They took my advice and camped on an island a few miles below Cotter. I really don't recall the number of scouts that made the trip, but I suppose near 20. Everything went off well the first day. The boys and their dads all caught fish. I would fish in a boat with two scouts for an hour, and then take two others, until we had done the entire group. The second day, we boated a lot of small trout, but with one group we caught one over seven pounds. With the very next group, we boated a six and a half pounder. The boys were really excited about the big ones. I asked the boys that helped land the two big trout if they would like to come on my TV show the next week and hold up the fish for the camera, which they did.

However, getting back to the river the second night, a severe thunderstorm passed over the island. The wind was so strong it blew down trees. It scattered tents and equipment all over the island. However, no one was hurt. We finished the trip with no further problems. After that, I never heard from any of them, until some 25 years later when I met this one eating lunch in a supermarket. He was surprised that I remembered the trip with the scouts and their dads. There is only one way to explain it! "Wings of Chance."

5

ONE OF THE earliest times I quail hunted with Sam Walton was east of Cassville, Missouri. Sam had called me and told me that Bob Hart, who worked for Wal-Mart, was a good quail hunter and wanted us to join him for a few days hunt. We arranged a date. I drove down to meet them in Cassville. Bob was there when I arrived, but Sam, at the last minute, had an emergency meeting of some kind. However, he was to come in the next day. Bob and I hunted that day; we found lots of birds and had a good hunt. Bright and early the next day, Sam arrived and we hunted two days. At that time, southwest Missouri offered some of the finest quail hunting anywhere. It was tough hunting, but in most cases the challenge was worth it. I hunted many more times with Sam. It seemed Bob and I could never get our hunting schedules together, but remained friends down through the years. Bob has been with Wal-Mart from the early days, down to the present time. He has been a store manager, a district manager, and had other duties. He was good for Wal-Mart, and Wal-Mart was good for him. Just recently, when I was at Wal-Mart's home office in Bentonville, Arkansas, I saw Bob and another longtime Wal-Mart man, Tom Coughlin. I was telling them about my new book and that David Glass had requested the first one off the press. Well, we will get number two and number three. Both of them have been with Wal-Mart a long time, and they both like to hunt.

Bob had a quail-hunting lease in Texas. A few years back, he invited me down for a quail hunt with him and his son. I told him that I would need to shoot a movie for my TV show and that I would like to bring my son-in-law, Dr. Jim Trotter, to help me. We arranged a date. He said that he and his son would be there early. We were to drive down for a few days. My son-in-law is a dentist in Overland Park, Kansas, and couldn't leave until 5 p.m. on Wednesday. We planned to leave at that time, drive all night, and be ready to hunt with Bob Thursday, Friday and Saturday, and drive back Sunday. I had my station wagon loaded, picked Jim up at 5:30, and we headed down I-35 toward Wichita. The weather forecast was not good, but we thought we could drive out of it. We hit the icing at Emporia, Kansas and the weather worsened. We were fortunate to have four-lane highways to Wichita Falls, Texas. It was touch and go all the way. We arrived in Wichita Falls about 1 a.m. and decided we had had enough. The freezing rain was even worse than it had been, but we were not far from Bob's place. We found a motel with a vacancy and decided to get some rest. We asked the night clerk to awaken us in two hours and we would try to make it the rest of the way. The lady didn't call us, and we slept until about 6 a.m. The weather was no better, but we decided to drive on to Albany. Bob's lease was not far from this small town. I had been driving most of the time and asked Jim if he could take over. I went to sleep. Just at the outskirts of Albany, Jim awakened me with a start and asked me if this engine ever heated up. I told him that it never had! He said, "Well, the light is on and something is wrong." There was an all-night service station at the edge of town. Jim pulled in and we jumped out. Ice about one-inch thick had formed at the radiator grill, cutting off all the air. The service station operator helped us remove the ice. He said, "I have never seen anything like that." I told him that I had driven in ice storms and blizzards thousands of miles and I had never seen anything like it, but I guess there's always a first time for everything! I had Bob's telephone number and called him from a pay phone. Bob and his son came into town to lead us to his lease. The weather didn't improve much, and we didn't have the kind of hunting Bob had planned for us. However, we did have a good hunt. What do I remember about this trip? Bob's great hospitality, icy roads and how close we came to destroying the engine of my trademark, my red Ford Country Sedan.

Back in the late '40s through the late '60s, there was no finer quail hunting than you could find in the northeast corner of Oklahoma, the southeast corner of Kansas, the northwest corner of Arkansas, and the southwest corner of Missouri. This four-state area, to me, was one of the truly great fun places to hunt quail. There may be places to hunt quail where you may find more birds, but I have never hunted an area that offered the challenge of those brushy hillsides in its prime days. It is not that way today, and it is not likely that it will ever be like that again. There is no way that I can picture with words the anticipation, the challenge, the excitement, the thrill and the satisfaction that came when hunting quail with a good bird dog in this type of terrain. Certainly, different people have different tastes; what excites and thrills me in quail hunting might not mean a thing to others. If someone were to ask me to tell them about one day's quail hunting that would stand out in my memory most, I would be hard-pressed to answer. In 60 years of quail hunting, in many parts of our country, my story of the good days would fill many books. One of the great things God gave man when he created him was the ability to remember the good times and to forget the stupid mistakes. For the life of me, I cannot remember my first fish, but I can remember the first quail I shot.

I was hunting with a guy named Nelson. His bird dog, a pointer, was named Lemon. I was using a borrowed gun, a 12-gauge double-barrel side-by-side. It was a bright November day. We were hunting along a small stream on some bottomland. I had never hunted quail, and after hunting hard for several hours with nothing I was losing interest. I found a pecan tree and found that eating pecans was more fun than hunting quail. Nelson and his dog Lemon were working a grassy field at the edge of the creek. I heard him yell, "Hold it, Lemon." Then I heard a couple of shots. Then I heard him yelling to Lemon, "Dead bird. Hunt dead." I thought how stupid I was to be eating pecans at the time the dog found a covey of quail. I walked sheepishly to them, but with no apologies. Nelson said, "When Lemon points another bird, I want you to shoot it; I'll just watch." He had seen where the birds had settled down, and soon the dog came down on a solid point. It was a fairly open spot, but near the creek. He told me to flush the bird and shoot. Any veteran hunter knows that the bird in the wild doesn't always fly where you want it to go. When you walk in behind the dog, the birds may come back over your head, go to the right or left, or go behind a tree, if one is close. That is why hunting birds in the wild is a greater challenge than hunting pen-raised birds — but getting back to that day in Oklahoma 60 years ago. Lemon hadn't been on point that long, but in my memory, he stands like a statue at the edge of the creek. We expected the bird to go straight ahead; instead it came out with a burst and turned sharply to the right across the creek past some trees. It was a difficult shot, but I killed it. Nelson was surprised, and I was surprised. Lemon didn't seem to think much about it, but brought the bird back to his master, who gave it to me. My first quail, and I was hooked! Little did I dream that 60 years later, and hundreds of quail hunting days, that I would be writing about Lemon and my first quail hunt.

One day, some 30 years ago, I was working in Bentonville, Arkansas. By chance, I met a friend of the family. I believe his name was Clanton. He asked me if I still hunted quail. I told him that I did and asked him why. He said, "I have a lot of quail on my farm and no one hunts them anymore." He lived several miles west of Bentonville. Years ago, it was a good quail hunting area, with a few small cornfields and fairly open land. I had wanted to take my wife's dad, M.H. Barnett, on a good quail hunt. He was 77 years old. His knees and legs were giving him a problem. There was plenty of good quail hunting close to where he lived near Stella, Missouri, but the terrain was not easy-going for a man his age. I thought this might be the right place to take him. We arranged a date and I drove down with the dogs. At that time, I was using three pointers: Old Country Squire, a new male pointer named Bill that I had bought from a hunter from Pea Ridge, Arkansas, and an old female pointer named Peggy. Not many dogs could find as many birds as Old Squire. Bill was just an average dog, and Peggy a little below average. However, Peggy was one of the best retrievers I ever owned. She would find more downed birds than most, and for that reason, I kept her around. It was some two hours drive from M.H.'s place to where we planned to hunt. It was a beautiful day for a hunt. We drove to Bentonville to get him a non-resident Arkansas hunting license, because I already had mine. Then we drove to Clanton's farm. We found lots of quail and had good dog work. The Clantons had a nice lunch for us. We let M.H. have a short rest and went back at it. By three o'clock, M.H. had done well and was only one short of his limit. I didn't shoot any of his birds for him, it was his day, but I had my limit. He was getting tired and said for me to shoot that one bird. I said, "No, M.H., I want you to get that last bird." He agreed to try. A short time later, Bill made a point at the edge of a blackberry thicket. The spot was about 30 yards past a newly built barbed wire fence. I said, "M.H., here's your chance." As he tried to crawl through the fence, he snagged his hunting coat and could not go either way. Bill was still holding his point, but Peggy was edging closer. Peggy didn't like to honor another dog's point. I just knew they were going to flush the bird.

M.H. said, "You shoot that bird, I'm hung up in the fence." I told him that I wasn't going to do it, and helped him through the fence. By this time, Peggy had her nose in front of Bill's, but the bird stayed put. M.H. walked in and flushed the bird, a single. He burst into the air and swung sharply to the left. It was a difficult shot, but M.H. dropped it. The bird fell in the dense blackberry thicket. I didn't think there was a chance to find it. I wanted to find that bird if it took the rest of the day. Peggy, bless her heart, stayed with it until she found it and brought it out of the thicket. When M.H. took the bird and he turned to me he had tears in his eyes, tears of triumph; he had shot his limit! It may not seem like much to others, but to a man at his age and in his physical condition, it was a great moment. I asked him if he wanted to come back the next day. He was excited about it, and Clanton said that he would be happy to have us, so we planned it and drove back to M.H.'s place. However, we didn't consider the weather. That night a cold-front passed through. When we got up it was cold and starting to sleet. M.H. said, "Harold, it's cold out there and I'm beat up! I won't be able to make it."

I decided to take a short hunt with my dogs, just walking from M.H.'s place. I knew all the neighbors and had permission to hunt. We had not gone a mile from the house when Country Squire ran over to a thicket at the edge of a field. Most good bird dogs, after hunting the same area, will learn and remember where they found birds. Squire knew that a covey of quail used that thicket at the edge of a field. He came down on a point. Bill and Peggy honored his point. That is always a beautiful sight for a hunter, to see his dogs solid on point. I had no one to share the moment. The sleet had stopped and I flushed the birds. It was a big covey. Three birds fell. The dogs retrieved two of them. Just when I thought they were not going to find the third bird, I turned to go to the wooded area to where I thought the rest of the covey might have landed. I had taken a few steps and felt something against my leg. It was Peggy. She had found the third bird and brought it to me. I took the bird and patted Peggy on head. The dog was as pleased as I was. When I reached the wooded area, two quail flushed back through the trees. I shot twice and missed both shots. It was getting much colder, with a strong wind out of the north. I decided the smart thing to do was start back toward the house and head for Kansas City.

As I came out of the wooded area, I had to pass the edge of a cornfield. The corn had not been picked. I did not want to walk through the standing corn. I saw Country Squire looking as if he were close to quail. Then he suddenly froze on point, right in the corn. The other dogs honored his point. I just assumed that it was a single bird from the covey. I walked in to flush the bird, and a big covey burst out all around me. People who have never hunted quail in the wild cannot understand what an explosive moment it is. I was startled, but managed to drop three birds. It was a thrill to find two big coveys within a short distance of each other, and I was less than a mile from the house. While I had missed two wild shots in the woods, I was feeling happy with dropping three birds on successive covey rises. However, the dogs only found two of the downed birds. I thought that it wasn't too bad; I had five birds, and started to the house. After a few steps, I felt something against my leg. It was Peggy with the third bird. I could hardly believe it. I dropped down on one knee, took the bird, and gave Peggy a big hug.

To reach the house, I had to cross a pasture of short grass. In my mind I was think-ing this was a great morning; I had six quail out of two covey rises, in less than an hour. I just lacked two birds of having my limit for the day, but was perfectly content with that. Halfway across the pasture, Bill came down on a point. I hadn't seen any birds from the last covey fly in that direction. I thought perhaps Bill had pointed a rabbit. By the way, I have never owned a good bird dog that didn't occasionally point a rabbit — but back to Bill. I was about 50 yards away when Bill made his point. Squire and Peggy honored his point. It was right out in open pasture and the grass cover was short. I walked up to Bill and was about to say, "Bill, come off that rabbit," when I saw the birds. There were two quail roosters snuggled down in the short grass. They were plainly visible. I'm sure that each of the three dogs could see them. The roosters had their heads in opposite directions. I just knew that one of them would go one way, and one would go the other. I had seen quail in front of a pointing dog on other occasions, but nothing so visible as that moment. How I wished for a camera, or a hunting buddy, to verify the scene. I stood there for a time and just savored the moment. I walked in to flush the birds, again expecting one to go one way and one the other. You won't believe it, but the bird facing east flew east and the other turned quickly in the air and followed it. I dropped both birds! That finished my limit, three birds on each two covey rises, and then a double. What a moment! It was a once-in-a-lifetime hunt, and no one to share it with me.

I walked back to the house. M.H. said, "You were not gone long. You must not have found any birds." I told him that I had shot my limit. He wouldn't believe it. I told him to look in my hunting coat. He was as amazed as I was and it just happened to me. I drove back to Kansas City with two hunts to remember. M.H. Shooting his limit in Arkansas, which turned out to be his last hunt, and my short hunt that morning. You could say, "The Wings of Chance had clearly blown our way."

6

FOR MANY YEARS I was on the banquet circuit, speaking to all kinds of groups all over the country. When I was called to speak to the faculty banquet of the University of Kansas, I thought I had it made. My mom always wanted to be proud of me. It was when I stood before the faculty members of the great University of Kansas at Lawrence that I wished Mom was there.

The next week, I was called to speak to the 14-state Funeral Directors Convention at Biloxi, Mississippi. I addressed many of the farm groups around the Midwest and many times found new places to hunt. I was speaking to Farm Bureau's Annual Meeting at Osborne, Kansas. Osborne is located in the central part of the state, right in the heart of great quail and pheasant hunting country. The president of the Farm Bureau owned a lot of land, but was not a hunter. In the course of the dinner meeting, I was asking him about the pheasant and quail population that year. He told me that he had seen a lot of birds on his land, and if sometime I was looking for a place to hunt, call him. I didn't think much about it at the time, but the next week when I was in Wichita producing my TV show, Webb Smith, the sportscaster at the TV station, asked me about a hunting trip. Webb was a good sportscaster and a real nice person. We had become friends through the years. I had been producing my nationally syndicated TV show there. Webb had 16-year-old twin boys who wanted to go hunting with me. Osborne, Kansas was about as close to Wichita as it is to Kansas City.

I thought of the Farm Bureau president and called him. He told me that they would be delighted to have me bring the twin boys to hunt. We arranged a date; Webb brought his twin boys, and Dusty and I drove out with our bird dogs. We hunted two days with the boys, but we hit two extremely warm November days. We didn't do as well as we expected. The boys couldn't stay another day. It was getting late in the afternoon when we got back to our vehicles.

We had just loaded the dogs in their crates when a neighbor came driving by. When he saw my station wagon with my name on it, he stopped his pickup. He asked my host what was going on. When he told him that we were there to shoot a hunting show for TV, he asked if he could see my dog, Country Squire. He said that he had seen him many times on TV. We visited for a while, and he asked our host how we had done. He told him that we hadn't done well. He asked if we had hunted his quarter section that was in the soil bank program. My host said, "No, we didn't hunt there because you had it posted with a No Hunting sign."

The neighbor asked us if we were going to stay over another day. He said, "I don't allow much hunting, but you guys are welcome to try it." It was too late to do much. The twins and Webb went back to Wichita. The three of us drove up to check out the soil plot, hoping to hunt it the next day. We stopped the station wagon just inside the gate and got out. Dusty slammed the car door shut, and pheasant flew out in every direction. We didn't even let the dogs out nor try to shoot, hoping for a good day on the morrow. You couldn't have found a better place to hunt: sweet clover about knee-high. It was perfect for our movie.

Dusty and I were staying at a motel in the little town of Downs, Kansas. We fed our dogs; we had two pointers, Country Squire and Maverick, and a pretty little setter named Susie. Dusty had his Labrador retriever. We had special crates for them in the back of the wagon. We ate a bite and went to bed. The weather was still nice outside, probably 60 degrees.

I awakened about 4:30 a.m. and I could hear the roar of the wind. I looked out the north window to the wagon. It was snowing like crazy. If you have never been in a blizzard on the prairie, it would be hard for you to visualize. The snow was coming straight across. It was wet and sticky. The west and north side of my station wagon had a blanket of wet snow about six inches thick, and on the ground, drifts all around. I awakened Dusty and told him we were in the midst of a blizzard and that we might not get our picture. I didn't like letting the dogs out to feed them, but I didn't have any choice. I turned on the radio; they said the wind chill was 27 degrees below zero. The snow let up some, but the cold wind didn't! We ate a bite and drove out to pick up our host. I wish I could remember his name. He was surprised that we planned to hunt, but bundled up and went with us.

Dusty was big and strong, and it fell his lot to carry the camera first. We drove to the soil bank area. The snow started coming again, and I mean it was going straight across, parallel with the ground, as only it can do on the prairie. You can imagine what it was like to walk through that tangled mess of uncut sweet clover in about six inches of snow. The pheasants sat tight, but the dogs worked beautifully. Once, Maverick pointed a coyote that was curled up asleep. The snow was getting deeper, but we were making progress with the picture. Country Squire made a point. Dusty yelled for me to come. Dusty had the camera going and told me to flush the bird. I did, and a hen pheasant came out. He yelled, "Don't shoot, it's a hen!" I looked back at Squire, he was still on point. He was standing belly-deep in snow, the rest of the dogs honoring his point. I walked in and a big rooster came thrashing out. We shot it. Dusty's Labrador made a beautiful retrieve. Dusty got the picture. We looked around and Squire was still on point. I said, "Two birds have come out of that sweet clover and snow." Dusty said, "Squire hasn't lied yet. You had better be ready and kick there again." Out came another rooster. We shot him and Dusty got it all on film!

Dusty said, "Dad, I've carried the camera this far, now it's your turn. So we just changed jobs and finished the movie. It may have been one of the best pheasant pictures we made for television. All because a friendly neighbor saw our station wagon on a country road and gave us permission to hunt his soil bank ground.

"Wings of Chance."

While I'm telling about western Kansas blizzards, I must tell you of a pheasant hunt we planned near Norton, Kansas. My next-door neighbor wanted to go hunting with us. At that time, Smokey, my oldest boy, was working for me. The three of us loaded up the dogs and gear and headed west on I-70 to Junction City, Kansas, where we took 18 Highway on to Hill City. The weather was nice until we got within some 50 miles of Hill City. It started snowing just before dark. When we arrived in Hill City, there was some eight to ten inches of snow, and still coming down. I was driving, and we started north out of Hill City. Visibility was so bad that I was trying to follow some fresh car tracks; I even opened my door and was just creeping along. I ended up in someone's back yard when they turned into their driveway. I told Smokey and my neighbor that we were turning back and would spend the night in Hill City. We finally found one small room in an old hotel for the three of us. It wasn't much, but better than sleeping in the car. We parked the car at curbside in front of the hotel. The next morning I looked out the window. My station wagon was completely buried, as were other parked cars. We had to shovel out and brush off before we could leave for Norton. Smokey took movies of us digging out.

We drove on to Norton to meet Clyde Ukele, the game warden, and a biology teacher from Kansas State University. I'm sorry that I cannot remember his name. We had hunted and fished many times with Ukele. He was a good outdoorsman and a nice guy. Before leaving Kansas for our trip, I had called Buddy Baier about buying a bird dog. My dogs had about run their course, and I wanted a new strong dog. Buddy told me that he had a big male pointer dog for sale. He told me that he ranged fast and wide and might not be what I wanted. I hunted hard and was young and strong. I told him I wanted a going Jesse! He told me to take the dog on a trip, and if the dog was too much for me, we would find another. We left my old dogs at home and took the new one.

We joined Ukele in Norton and drove to the special spot he had saved for us. There must have been 10 inches of new snow. The ground was not frozen underneath, and walking was going to be a tough go. We stopped the cars on a spot that was solid. Ukele let his dogs out. We got the cameras out. Smokey had the camera before I let the new dog out. I asked the rest of the men to watch the dog while I got my shotgun. I turned the dog loose and reached in the car to get my shotgun. I had hardly turned my back on the dog when he took off. I said, "Men, where's my dog?" It was nowhere to be seen, but I could see his tracks in the snow. I told Smokey to start hunting with the rest of them, that I would try to track the dog. The biologist had his dog, a Weimariner, that stayed right at his heels. He said, "I will go with you and help you find the dog." We took off following the tracks. It was really tough walking with the snow and wet muddy fields.

We had gone at least a quarter of a mile when we saw the dog on a point. We made it to about 60 yards from the dog, and out came a rooster pheasant. It was just out of range, and the pointer took off after the bird. The pheasant flew on about a quarter of a mile and set down in the snow. The pointer was after the bird and pointed it again. We struggled through the muck again, and about the time we were within shooting range the pheasant flushed again. We saw it land in snow about another quarter of a mile. It was about all I could take, but I was determined to get the dog. I wasn't worried about the bird. That time the pheasant landed in some high weeds in a draw and held tight. The dog pointed the bird and his dog honored the point.

We prepared to walk in. I thought after this long chase, I'm going to show the biologist how quick I can shoot. We walked in, the bird flushed. I came down on it, pulled the trigger, and heard it snap! I had failed to load my gun at the car. The biologist shot the pheasant and his dog retrieved it, but I caught the pointer by the collar and held on. I didn't want another chase. We finally made it back to the car. Smokey and Ukele had the movie half made. I put the dog in its crate. We hunted the rest of that day and the next, made our movie and headed home. I took the pointer back to Buddy and bought a beautiful white setter to go with my older dogs. I wasn't as young as I thought!

"Wings of Chance."

While I was writing about these two blizzards, the phone rang. It was my son Dusty. He had planned to drive to Sidney, Nebraska on a business trip. They called him from Sidney to tell him of a bad blizzard and some of the roads were closed. I said, "Dusty, I was just writing about blizzards on the prairie."

"Wings of Chance."

When I think of pheasant hunting, I immediately remember two trips with a baseball twist. I don't know exactly what the year was, but I received a call from Runt Marr, former St. Louis Cardinal scout. At that time, Runt and his wife lived on Grand Lake in Oklahoma near Long's Dock; the first heated dock built anywhere, to my knowledge. Before Long's heated dock was built, my wife and I caught lots of crappie off Runt's boat dock. Runt was famous for signing some great baseball players. Among those that I remember were Boyer brothers: Cloyd, who pitched for the Cardinals, and Kenny, who was their star third baseman. I had known Runt and his wife from my baseball days, when Runt was president of the Joplin Miners in the Western Association. I had never known Runt to hunt, but had fished with him many times after he retired to Grand Lake. Runt was a friend of Burleigh Grimes, the Brooklyn Dodgers famous "spit-ball pitcher." Burleigh may have been the last pitcher in the major leagues to be allowed to throw the spit-ball.

Burleigh had called Runt about a pheasant-hunting trip to South Dakota. He and a friend named Sewell, from the Baltimore Orioles, had hired a guide in some little town in North Central, South Dakota. Runt called and asked if I would like to meet them there and shoot a pheasant-hunting movie. I was delighted with the opportunity to hunt with Runt, and also to meet Burleigh Grimes. I wish I could remember the name of the town where we made our headquarters. I think it was near the city of Mitchell; anyway, it was in the heart of pheasant country. The weather was typical of November in South Dakota. Pheasants were everywhere! Most people who hunt today would hardly believe the number of birds. I did not hunt it in its prime, but it was still unbelievable when we were there. Runt had hired a native guide and made all the arrangements for our stay. I'll never forget driving around the cornfields in the mornings before the hunt. Time after time, we would drive past a draw with a few trees; you could see 15 or 20 roosters in a tree. What a magnificent sight, with the sun shining on their brilliant color. God didn't make anything for the hunter in the field that was any more beautiful. We couldn't start hunting until noon, so we had lots of time to hear Runt and Burleigh spin yarns about the years of the old-time professional baseball players in action.

Smokey and I carried cameras most of the time. One afternoon, we were making a draw between two cornfields. I was following Runt and Smokey was following Burleigh with the guide. Runt was in the edge of the draw in grass and weeds up to his waist. I yelled at him that a bird was coming his way. I had the camera on him and the bird. He was swinging on that bird when two more came into the picture. Runt switched birds and about five more rosters came onto the scene. Runt switched birds again. So many roosters came out over Runt that he switched from one bird to another and never got off a shot. The movie came out beautifully showing the whole bit. Burleigh really gave Runt the raspberry.

The next day, we were going to work a big cornfield. My son Smokey followed the hunters through the field, and the guide and I, with one other hunter, went to the other end of the field to block. Pheasants were going in every direction, with lots of shooting going on. Runt and Burleigh were almost to us when the game warden drove up. He was checking everyone for their birds and their licenses. Everyone checked out fine but Runt. He was going through his billfold and fumbling with papers. He had bought his license but couldn't find it. Burleigh turned to the game warden and said, "Why don't you take the little s.o.b. in, he never buys a license!" That's a real friend for you. Runt found his license and everything was all right. They had their limit just coming through the field.

The guide said to the landowner, "Why didn't you let us hunt that field back of your house?" He told them he was saving it for Harold and Smokey! He told us to get ready, that they would drive around the field and flush the birds over us. I gave Smokey my 12-gauge and picked up what I thought was my wife's 20 gauge. The farmer had told us to go to the fence back of the barn. Smokey yelled at me to hurry, that birds were already flushing our way. I was trying to load my gun as I ran and couldn't get the shells in. I looked and saw that I didn't have my wife's 20-gauge, but had my 28-gauge quail gun. Here I was with roosters all over me and no shells. I remembered that I might have left some 28s under my front seat, from dove hunting. Smokey was shooting birds and yelling at me. I found five or six 28-gauge shells with number eight shot. I ran to the fence by Smokey. It looked like the world had turned into pheasants. Roosters were coming over us in droves, some as low as 20 yards. In a matter of minutes, we had our limit of birds, right by the farmer's barn. Never in my lifetime had I ever seen anything like it, and never expect to see it again. I'm sure at times we had a hundred roosters over us at the same time.

"Wings of Chance."

The state of Nebraska called and wanted me to do some hunting in their state with the possibility of promoting it on radio and television. Arrangements were made for my wife and me to go there for a quail hunt with Gene Hornbeck of Omaha, who worked

Pheasant hunting in Nebraska with Gene Hornbeck.

with the Fish and Game Commission. He had invited a hunter, Rand Horsely, to bring his dogs for a hunt. Rand had field trial dogs and quite a reputation as a hunter. I can't remember the name of the town where we met the two of them.

My wife Bonnie had become an excellent quail shooter, and I think she surprised them. She also handled the camera while I hunted. We had three good days and made a movie for television. During the course of the hunt, Gene asked why I didn't come back to shoot a sharp-tailed grouse story. I was raised in prairie chicken country and as a boy had shot a couple of shows in the Flint Hills near El Dorado, Kansas. I told Gene that I didn't have time to do it, with the commitments I had already made, but would like to plan it for the next year. That is, provided the Lord let us live that long. He did, and the next year we arranged for a sharp-tailed grouse hunt with Gene in the sand hills of Nebraska. I told Floyd Roberts about it. He was the manager of Sporting Goods at Sears Cleveland Avenue Store, who were my sponsors on radio. He had taught school in western Nebraska at one time, and would certainly like to make the trip. He said, "I'll carry your camera and help you with the driving. However, I'd like to take my gun along, just in case I might get to hunt."

I don't remember the name of the town where we met Gene. He had made arrangements for us to stay at a motel, there and he brought Rand Horsely and his dogs for the hunt. The weather was beautiful. Just right for our movie-making. We drove out to the hill country. Rand let his pointers out and they took off. They were out of sight in a matter of minutes. Rand said, "We had better follow." I handed Floyd the movie camera, grabbed my shotgun, and the four of us started after the dogs. If you have ever hunted in the sand hills, you know how much territory you have to cover. We made it down the first ridge. Floyd turned to me and said, "I can't make it any farther, and my old ticker won't make it." We took him back to the car.

Sharp-tailed grouse hunting in Nebraska.

I left my gun and picked up the camera. We had a good hunt and got the movie started. We hunted another day and a half and we had the movie made. We went back to our cars. I told Gene I would like to take time away from the camera and hunt a little bit. Rand said, "Let's go to another spot." I followed them, and when I got out of the car with my gun, Rand laughed and told me that as they were driving to the spot. Gene told him that he'd had enough, but he wasn't going to let that city dude walk him down. We got into birds right quick, and I got to do my first sharp-tail shooting. Rand and Gene had to leave the next day, but arranged for the two of us to hunt ducks. Since Floyd had been unable to walk and hunt sharp-tails, he could get a day's hunt in the duck blind.

We got up early the next day and went out to a lake near town, where they had arranged for us to hunt. We had shot several ducks. About 2 a.m., as we sat in the duck blind, Floyd said, "Man, would I like to see that KU—K-State football game tomorrow in Lawrence. If we would leave now and drive all night, we could make it." I said, "Why didn't you say something last night?" He told me that he would buy me the biggest steak in Grand Island on the way, and he would do the driving. I had a piece of plywood on 2x8s, with an air mattress, and sleeping bag in the back of the station wagon. When we made long trips, one of us could sleep in comfort while the other drove. I told him that we had to dress our ducks and check out of the motel.

It was dark when we made it to Grand Island. He did buy me a big steak, and they do have good steaks in Nebraska! He was familiar with the roads, as he had spent several years in the area. After dinner, I got into my sleeping bag to get some shuteye. It seemed that I had just dropped off to sleep when I heard tires screaming and the station wagon bouncing around. Floyd had gone to sleep at the wheel and run off the highway. Fortunately, it was on level ground with a wide ditch. No harm done. I rolled out of my bunk and drove the rest of the way to Kansas City. Floyd made it in time for his football game, and I made it in time to get the film to the processor.

"Wings of Chance."

7

To MY KNOWLEDGE, when I was a youngster in western Kansas nobody hunted doves. My first experience with doves occurred in northwest Arkansas. A man from Texas had bought a piece of property near Bentonville, Arkansas. I heard a lot of shooting one day; duck season was not open and quail season was not open, I couldn't understand what was causing all the commotion. The hunters had surrounded a small pond and were shooting the doves as they came in for water. I didn't think too much about it at the time, but when I came to Kansas City I learned that doves were a great game bird. Besides being an elusive winged target, doves are good to eat.

Some people are a little touchy about hunters shooting doves, yet God put them here for food, as he did the quail and pheasant. If I wanted to train a youngster to be a good winged shot, I would put him near a waterhole or feed lot with a couple of boxes of shells, and let him bang away to his hearts content. Some folks might say doves are too tough a target for a youngster. However, on a pheasant hunt or a duck hunt, they might get to shoot at five or six targets. In dove hunting, they would get birds coming in at all angles and might get 25 or 30 shots. The same is true of teaching a youngster to fish with artificial lures; I would start them on crappie rather than bass. On crappie, they would be given many more opportunities to learn to feel a fish take an artificial lure.

We have two stories to share with you about dove hunting, in order to tell you about a deer-hunting trip to Wyoming.

Hunters in the south, especially Texas, have hunted doves for years. Many hunters travel to Mexico to hunt there. However, there are parts of the country where people are a little sensitive about it. Really, there is no difference hunting doves than hunting ducks or quail. In fact, God fed the children of Israel quail in the wilderness in the long ago.

In the early years of television, I tried to be discreet with hunting shows, but finally decided to show a dove hunting picture. I had used many quail, pheasant, duck and goose hunting movies on my TV series. Back in those days, the TV station kept the switchboard open until closing. I do not remember if they shut down at midnight. My show ran from 9:00 to 10:00 on Monday nights at that time. After the show, the switchboard would light up. Many nights it would be an hour or better for me to take all the calls. Most of the calls were people wanting to know about places to fish or hunt. The night I ran the dove-hunting movie, a young law student, Kenny Grabmiller, was working the night shift at the switchboard. After the show, I stood by answering calls. I noticed Kenny was having a bit of trouble with a caller. When I became free, I asked Kenny to let me take the call. It was from a lady viewer who was disturbed about the dove hunting. She said, "Harold Ensley, I used to love you, but I hate you now, shooting those innocent little doves!"

I asked her if she ate chicken. She said, "Yes, and I wish I had some fried chicken right now!" I told her that the same God made the chicken that made the doves. Then she admitted that should make it right. After she hung up, I asked Kenny if she had given him a bad time. He said, "Harold, you are going to get a kick out of this. When she started airing her problem with dove hunting, I asked her if she was a vegetarian. She said, "No, I'm a Methodist.' " End of story!

During the early years of our TV series, the television audience was sensitive about showing big game hunting. I had no qualms about shooting a deer or antelope for meat. God created them for us to eat. However, I don't care to watch the animal being shot on the TV screen. Producing a 30-minute live TV show, 52 weeks a year, required constant searching for program material. We shot many shows of upland game hunting and waterfowl hunting, but never devoted much time to big game hunting. We made several trips to the Rockies in Utah, New Mexico, Colorado and Wyoming, but mostly shot the scenery going in, the camping and the scenery coming out. We want to share a few of them with you. The stories will not necessarily be in chronological order.

A friend of mine, John Dumolt, of the Kansas City Police Department, and I were dove hunting east of Kansas City one afternoon. John shot a double. He shot one bird going one way, and one going in the opposite direction. He was standing knee high in weeds. I yelled at him to mark the spot where the birds had fallen and I would come help him. He threw his cap down where he thought the first bird fell. He then went to get the second bird. We laugh about it today, because we found both birds, but never found his cap.

John and I had hunted and fished together many times. Late one August he called me about a deer and antelope hunt in Wyoming. He, Herb Bansbacher, another policeman, and a friend, Bill Koonze, had planned a trip and wanted me to go with him. Bill and Herb were going to drive on ahead to set up camp; John and I were to leave after my TV show, drive all night and meet them at camp. We were to meet their guide, Glenn Allison, in Casper, Wyoming, and he would lead us to the camp. We met Glenn and bought our hunting licenses.

I asked Glenn if there was a trout stream near the camp where I might fish a bit. He told me there was a small stream not too far from camp that had trout. I asked him what lures I should buy for trout. I had my ultra-light spinning gear with me, but at that time I had not learned to use crappie jigs for trout. He suggested that I get a couple of Panther Martins, a spinner bait with a fly. I hadn't planned to spend much time fishing, so I just got two of them, one of them with a gold blade and one with black. I think the lures were 1/16 oz.

We left Casper, following Glenn in his jeep. I had to drive like crazy to keep him in sight. We were headed for camp, which was in the Powder River, Crazy Woman area. We drove past the famous Hole in the Wall of Butch Cassidy, Sundance Kid fame. When we arrived at camp a little past noon, I asked Glenn what he had under the hood of that

Jeep. He told me that most of the guides would buy a new Jeep and then put a new Ford V8 motor in it. Bill and Herb had set up the tents and made the camp ready. First thing, they asked me if I brought my fishing tackle. They wanted some trout. Allen told them that he would take the Jeep and put them each on a deer stand. He and I would drive to the creek to fish. He later would pick them up.

When Allen and I reached the small stream, I could hardly believe the situation. It was a small stream, but the shallow pools looked good to me. He asked me if he could use one of my ultra-lite spinning outfits. He took one of the Panther Martins, tied it on the 2 lb.-test line, and started fishing in the shallow pools. I cannot remember whether he chose the black or the gold spinner. In short order, he had landed several rainbows, no large fish, but just right to take back to camp. I tied on the other Panther Martin and followed him. I think he had caught ten when I caught my first one. I thought this guy was one of the best trout fishermen I'd been around. I'm sure he thought I wasn't much of a fisherman. He looked at his watch and told me that he had to go get the hunters, but for me to go ahead and fish until he came back for me.

When he left, I picked up the rod he was using. By the time he returned, I had caught a nice string of trout. Whether the black blade or the gold blade made the difference, I'll never know. However, the one he was using worked, and the one I had didn't! I'm glad he didn't take it with him, or I would have never known the difference. The hunters didn't have a deer, but were very happy with the thought of trout for breakfast. The next day we did have fish for breakfast, with fried potatoes and eggs.

After breakfast, Allen drove Bill, John and me to a spot near a canyon a few miles from camp. Herb had stayed to clean up the breakfast mess. I was carrying my movie camera, Bill and John had their rifles, and Allen had his spotting scope, but no rifle. There was a grassy plateau on three sides of a canyon, which at that point was about 400 yards wide. It was just a deep canyon, possibly 200-foot cliffs at both sides. As we approached the edge of the canyon, we spotted two big bucks at the base of the cliff, about three or four hundred yards away. I yelled at John to shoot, and he couldn't see the buck's outline against the cliff. I handed John my camera and asked for his rifle. I dropped to one knee and fired. Bill was in a prone position firing away. The deer were so far away that they didn't even hear the shots we fired. The one I fired at climbed up out of the canyon and was a silhouette against the sky.

I asked Allen to check the distance on his spotting scope. He said, "It's a good 400 yards." I asked John about his rifle. He told me the scope was set for 300 yards. The deer was still standing there motionless. I pressed the trigger and the deer fell. Allen got the Jeep and drove us around the canyon to where the deer had fallen. The buck, a mule deer, had a beautiful rack. It looked more like an elk rack than a deer, with the diameter size of the antlers. It had six points on one side and five on the other. We took it back to camp and after lunch went back to get Bill and John a deer. We saw several trophy bucks, but didn't score.

The next day, Allen told us we would search for trophy antelope. It was the last day for John and me, but Bill and Herb were going to stay a few more days. We were not in high country, just grasslands, with a few areas of rough terrain. You could drive over most of it in a Jeep. As we drove around, we passed up several antelope, but no big herds, such as I have seen in other areas of Wyoming. When we saw a buck, the others would say, "Let's pass this one and look for a nicer trophy buck."

At noon, we hadn't fired a shot. Allen parked the Jeep on the south slope of a ridge overlooking a large grassland area. He had packed some sandwiches for us to eat while he took his binoculars and walked to the top of the ridge overlooking the north slope. He came back to the Jeep, put his binoculars away, and calmly told us there was a nice buck out on the open flat to the north. Nobody said anything, so I said I'd take him. He said it was going to be a hard stalk, for the antelope was in an open area of several thousand acres of grass. He said there was no cover except a narrow ravine leading to a small earthen dam. He told us that we could drive within a mile of the buck and that I could sneak up the ravine to the earthen dam. The altitude wasn't bad, about 9,000 feet. At that time, I had been jogging five or fix miles a day and thought that it would be a breeze. John got out with me and the guide drove the others about a mile past the ravine, in case the antelope spooked and headed that way. Crouching low, John and I started our stalk to the earthen dam. We were soon huffing and puffing our way.

When I thought I was in range, I eased up the side of the slope to see if the buck had been spooked. John followed at my side, but without a gun. We could see the animal plainly, but it was standing alertly, watching the others in the Jeep about a mile away. John whispered for me to shoot. He said that it was only about 300 yards. I straightened up and aimed the rifle, but was so out of breath I couldn't keep it in the scope. John was getting louder in his effort to get me to shoot; I was afraid the buck would hear us. He kept saying, "He's in range; shoot!" I told him there was no use to shoot when I couldn't hit it.

We crouched down and moved closer. John was about 50 yards behind me when I reached the earthen dam. I sat down for a short time to get my breath, and then eased up the side of the dam to where I thought I could see. I looked out across where the antelope was supposed to be and saw nothing. I immediately thought that it had spooked when John was trying to get me to shoot. About that time, the antelope stood up about 150 yards away, but facing the direction of the Jeep. Its ears were twitching, and you could tell that it was getting ready to take off. I dropped down on one knee in position to shoot, but all I could see was the animal's rear-end. It moved a little to one side, and through the scope I could see the edge of its shoulder blade. I pressed the trigger and the buck fell. I didn't move, but sat ready in case the animal got up and took off.

John came up and said, "Where is he?" In the grass you could see nothing. About that time, Allen and the others drove up. They had been watching through the binoculars. Allen said, "You must have hit him good because he dropped instantly." Allen was the first one to examine the antelope. He said, "Man, what a shot! You hit him right between the eyes!" Evidently, just as I shot, the buck turned in my direction and the bullet took him right between the eyes. I was shooting at his shoulder from behind. How lucky can you get?

"Wings of Chance."

I got my trophy mule deer at an estimated 400 yards, and my antelope at 125 steps! I walked it off myself to be sure. It was just the opposite of what you would expect. The next day, John and I drove home and the others followed later. I had the deer mounted, and for years it graced the wall above the fireplace in the TV studio. Sadly, I can't find one picture of that beautiful trophy.

8

IN THE FALL of 1953 a man named Morley Davies was transferred from Denver, Colorado, to Kansas City. He had been the Denver regional representative for J. Walter Thompson Advertising Agency. Upon arriving in Kansas City, he chanced to see my TV show on KCMO-TV, the CBS affiliate. He immediately called the station and asked for the right of first refusal to buy the show for the Ford Dealers of the Metropolitan Kansas City Area. The program was sponsored by a local firm, and after 13 weeks it proved to be too much for their advertising budget. Morley bought the show, and Ford kept it for almost 25 years. He liked the outdoors. He was a hunter and fisherman. He also was a great camper. I really think he preferred camping and cooking to fishing or hunting. We soon built a friendship that lasted as long as he lived. We had many good trips together, both hunting and fishing. We made a trip to Grand Lake in Oklahoma to fish for crappie, and we made a float trip on White River for trout. When he was promoted to J. Walter's office in Detroit, Michigan he had me fly there once for a muskie picture, and once for an ice-fishing picture at Houghton Lake.

While he was working the Denver office, Cedar City, Utah was in his district. The Ford dealer there was a great deer hunter. He and his family owned a mesa above Cedar City that covered some 33,000 acres of grassland. He wanted us to come out to shoot a deer-hunting movie. We made the necessary arrangements and started planning the trip. Morley had the camping gear. I bought a new 30.06 caliber deer rifle with a four-power scope. Morley had a 270 with a scope. He wanted to take his 16-year-old son, Richard. I told him it would be fine with me. Morley bought enough groceries for a month. We loaded my Ford and made ready to head west.

Back then, we had no way of taping my TV show, but I could tape my daily radio shows, which I did. My TV show was from 9:30 to 10:00 on Monday nights. We decided it would be best to leave when I got off the air and drive all night. Cedar City was 1,300 miles away. I drove the first part of the night, being familiar with the roads to Denver, and Morley was used to the roads to Cedar City. The weather was nice, and we made it in about 26 hours. This mesa had been the property of the Ford dealer's family since the days of the early settlers. It was typical southwest semi-arid land, but capable of handling sheep. It was situated above Cedar City. From a high point on the southern edge you could see Zion National Park. From an angle, you could see Bryce Canyon. If my memory serves me right, on a clear day you could see the outline of the north rim of the Grand Canyon. What a thrill just to get to camp surrounded by such spectacular beauty. At the edge of the mesa, there were timbered spots. There were some of the largest Aspen trees I had ever seen. I took pictures of my Ford station wagon coming down a dirt road among Aspen trees, 12 to 16 inches through at the base, and 40 to 50 feet high. The Ford dealer had a log cabin near the ascent to the mesa, but we had a tent. This was always Morley's big thing, setting up camp; and he liked to cook and also liked to eat!

After setting up camp and shooting some preliminary scenery shots, we took a short hunt. That first evening Morley, his son Richard, and I went for a short hunt. The weather was unseasonably warm, and the territory was new to us. Consequently, we just had a long walk. The second and third days were pretty much the same, but we ventured out farther from camp. Friday night the Ford dealer, his chief mechanic, and his son came up to join us. His mechanic was touted to be the best deer hunter in the area. His son was a big husky college lad. He was on the Utah State football team.

The weather was still almost like summertime. Saturday morning we made a short run, with nothing! Back at the cabin he said, "This afternoon we are going after a trophy buck." He told us that we would make a drive off the mesa in the timber along the southern slope. Then we would have three guys drive to a spot to block, and the rest of us would fall off the mountain to the valley below to drive the deer toward the blockers. I asked him if I could go with him and his son on the drive. He looked at me as though I were a tenderfoot and would just be in the way. Morley's boy wanted to go along. Rather reluctantly, he told us to get our rifles. We climbed to the highest point on the mesa where he separated us about 100 yards apart and motioned for us to fall off the ridge to the timber below in the valley. When he said, "fall off," it was almost that way. I honestly believe he was trying to test me! The slope of that mountain was between 45 and 60 degrees of loose volcanic ash and big boulders. Sometimes you had to grab a sapling or a tree and slide on down.

We soon were separated. I was bouncing from one boulder and came face to face with a big wildcat. To this day, I can still see that cat! I don't know if it was a big bobcat or a young mountain lion. I scared the cat and it scared me! The cat gave a big hiss and took off. At the moment, I was too busy to shoot. I came to my senses and took off after it. If I remember right, there was a $40 bounty on them. That's what they charged us for a non-resident hunting license. I went bouncing from boulder to boulder and ran into a nice buck. It surprised both of us and the buck took off. It disappeared below me in the Aspens. I kept going to a position where I could cover anything that crossed the opening about 100 yards below me. Through the Aspen, I could see the legs of the deer. The deer came out into the opening and stopped to look back. I shot and the deer dropped. The bullet had hit between the shoulder blades, as I shot it from above. The other three hunters heard the shot and came to me. It was not a big buck, eight-point, but I was happy. It was the first deer I had seen in three days. We dressed the deer out and the mechanic said, "We'll come back and get it in the morning." I said, "No, with that cat around it might not be here in the morning! Let's drag it up the road and bring the pickup to take it to camp."

The young football player handed his rifle to his dad. He put the deer across his shoulder and carried it about 100 feet. We were at about 9,000 feet elevation, and it was extremely warm. The incline up the hill was probably 45 to 50 degrees. His dad then carried the deer about 50 feet. It was my turn. I carried and dragged it about 20 feet. It was that way all the way up the slope to the road at the top of the mesa. At that time, I was jogging and running four or five miles a day. I had thought that I was in pretty good physical condition. However, the altitude and the warm temperature just about did me in! I was almost to the point of just leaving the deer and my rifle and just crawl the rest of the way. However, we made it to the road. The football player had finished the job, but passed out completely when we reached the road. The other hunters brought the pickup. They had a jug of water and we revived him. The others, who had been blocking the drive, had a nice buck. We made it back to camp and hung the deer in the shade, hoping that the cool desert air that night would keep them. We fixed our dinner and hit the sack.

About 2 a.m., I was awakened by a loud clap of thunder. I eased out of my sleeping bag and peeked out. Lightning was flashing across the sky. It started raining, then turned to sleet and snow. When we got up the next morning it was snowing like crazy and had already accumulated about eight inches on the ground. The man in charge of the sheep told us we had better get off the mesa. He said, "Snow will be up to the eaves on the cabin by late tonight. We are already moving the sheep to lower elevations. There are 10,000 sheep ahead of you on the road down the mountain." He said that while the sheep were like a sea of animals, the dogs could move them over. We packed our things and started down the mountain over the winding dirt road. It was a spectacular sight to see that many sheep and the dogs working them. I had Morley drive, and I filmed the whole procession.

We made it down to the lower elevations and soon drove out of the snow. Morley knew the country and the roads. He drove to Dillon, Colorado just before you go over Loveland Pass. We stopped at Dillon to get gas and it started to rain.

Morley said, "You had better put on your chains before we go over the pass." I told him I didn't have any chains. He said, "Buy some and have them put on!" I listened to him, although there was no snow at Dillon. I started driving slowly up the mountain, with cars zipping past me. Soon I realized why I needed chains. The snow started falling, cars were pulling off to put on chains. Soon we were on snow-packed roads with cars and trucks off in the ditch. We eased our way through the stalled traffic and made it over the pass. There must have been a hundred cars and trucks stalled on the two sides of the pass. We ran out of snow as we reached the lower elevations.

When we arrived in Denver, I realized that I was running out of time. My TV show was at 9:30 p.m., and my radio show was at 5 p.m. I called the television station to tell them I was running close on time and to get the studio ready. I told them to tell the radio crew that I would plan to stop somewhere to do the radio show from a phone booth. Morley said that he was too tired to drive and was afraid to let his 16-year-old son drive. It's a good road and a straight shot through Kansas to Kansas City. We took off. We made it to Salina in time to do my radio show from a phone booth. We arrived in Kansas City with enough time to change clothes, shave and do my TV show, live. It had been a wild and wonderful week! Typical of our schedule throughout the hunting season, for 48 years!

Wings of Chance!

IT WOULD TAKE A ROOM FULL OF BOOKS
TO COVER THE AMERICAN HUNTERS HERITAGE!!!!

From the days of the pilgrims, and the rest of the early settlers across the Alleghenies to Kentucky, along the east coast to the winning of the west, on the prairie and the mountains, wild game played an important part in American History. It mattered not whether it was wild turkey or deer, even the lowly rabbits and squirrels, it helped supply the family larder. God put them here for our food!

My first deer was taken in Utah and my first antelope was taken in New Mexico. Dale Motley was one of the pioneer resort operators on Lake of the Ozarks. His place, called Motley's Clear Water Resort, was located on the Big Niangua Arm. He was a good operator, and also my reporter from that section of the lake for my radio show. I fished with him many times, and in later years shot several fishing shows for TV. He was located in some of the best walleye and bass fishing on the lake. He also had one of the first and best heated crappie fishing docks on the lake. He had a friend who owned a big ranch in New Mexico. He had been asking Dale to come to his place to hunt antelope. The rancher was not that much of a hunter, nor was Dale. Somehow, he persuaded Dale to bring me out to film an antelope hunt. We finally decided to give it a try. If my memory serves me right, Dale and I flew to Amarillo, Texas, where his rancher friend met us and drove us to his ranch.

I learned a long time ago that distance doesn't mean much to those people. It was quite a drive to his ranch, but it was through a part of New Mexico I had never seen. His ranch was a working cattle ranch and covered several thousand acres of grassland. He had a lot of cattle, but he also had a good-sized herd of antelope. There wasn't much in the way of scenery, but we spent the first day taking our preliminary pictures. We saw several antelope. We came upon a herd with one big buck. It ran alongside our vehicle at top speed. It was just right for a spectacular camera angle. I was thrilled to be so lucky. However, at that time I was using an Eastman K100 movie camera with a turret and three lenses. It was not a reflex camera, so you were looking through the viewfinder and not the lens. We had been driving on dusty roads. I had lost my lens caps, so I just stuffed some Kleenex in the telephoto lens to protect it from dust. It wasn't until I went to reload my camera that I noticed the paper in the lens. I was heartsick that I had messed up the best scenes that we had on the whole trip. It just wasn't our day.

A short time later, the rancher ran over a boulder and tore the oil pan off his wife's Cadillac. I'll never forget, he stepped out of the car, saw the oil pouring out and said, "Let's leave it and go get my pickup." It was quite a walk, but we made it and finished out the day in his pickup.

The next day Dale and I each got our antelope and came home. I remember three things about the trip: messing up on one of the best camera shots I ever had, the rancher hitting the rock with his wife's Cadillac, and how fast an antelope can run. Proof again that the "Winds of Chance" blow from all directions!

In the early days of television, there seemed to be a bond between the performers and the audience that we do not have today. There were three networks, and in most cases, one television set for the entire family. Almost daily I meet people who say: "I watched your show when I was a child. On Saturday nights at 6 p.m. my dad called the family together around the television set to watch you." It isn't that way today, with 70 to 100 channels, and a TV set in every room.

For the first few years, the Kansas City Ford dealers sponsored my weekly show. We had a working relationship that was almost like family. I personally knew each one of the dealers and their families. I fished and hunted with those who love to fish and hunt. In 1959 the Kansas City District Ford dealers bought my show. There were 250 dealers in the district, ranging from the Colorado through Kansas to western Missouri, then south to northwest Arkansas and northeast Oklahoma. I don't think there was a city where each of these 250 dealers operated that I did not make a public appearance. I spoke to farm groups, soil conservation groups, civic clubs, high schools and colleges. It was a great opportunity to meet the people who paid the bills. I found the Ford dealers and their families to be an important part of the community. They were a class act, and it was an honor to serve them. I wish I had the time and space to mention each one individually. That would be impossible, but I want to mention a few special occasions.

In the mid '60s I received a call from Ray Davis, the Ford dealer in Syracuse, Kansas. At that time, each year a group of families from Syracuse would band together for a fishing trip to Lake Ogallala in western Nebraska. Each family pulled their own boat. Some had RVs and others had camping gear. They formed a caravan, all going together in a line that stretched almost from Syracuse to the Nebraska line. They were accompanied by a Kansas highway patrolman, who escorted the group across the

Walleye fishing in Ogallala with Howard Phifer, Ford dealer from Ulysses, Kansas.

state. Ray asked me if Dusty and I would join them and fish with them on Lake Ogallala. We arranged a date and joined the caravan at Goodland, Kansas. Everyone arrived safely at Lake Ogallala and we set up camp. It was our first time to be with these people and gave us an opportunity to make a lot of new friends. Some people fished, some got on water skis, and some just went boating. Everyone was doing his or her own thing. Dusty and I fished with different ones, but could not possibly make the complete round. However, I never once heard anyone complain that we didn't fish with them. They just simply had a good old-fashioned get-together. This was America! Everyone just took it for granted. It was a way of life. For the first time in years, after the disaster in New York on September 11, 2001, it made us realize what we have and what we stand to lose!

But back to Nebraska. The weather was great and those of us who fished caught lots of fish. Oddly enough, I caught an 11-1/4-lb. walleye, the largest I caught anywhere. Everyone had good walleye and white bass fishing. Some crappie were caught, and also some small-mouth bass. The Ogallala Chamber of Commerce catered a big dinner at Lakeside for us one evening. They planned a return trip for the following year and made it an annual event. The next year, the day before departing they had a big street sale. They put a huge sign across Highway 50 with letters three feet high saying: Syracuse has gone fishing with Harold Ensley! At that time, Highway 50 went right down Main Street. They stretched the sign across the street from a second-story building on each side of the street. At that time, our programs just reached seven states. Tourists coming through town would say, "Who's Harold Ensley that the town goes fishing with him?" Dusty and I made the trip with them for several years. It was a great experience, and our sincere thanks to the nice people of Syracuse, Kansas.

About that time, speaking of "Wings of Chance," I received a call from Texas. It was a rancher named George Light. He owned a big spread south of San Antonio and had decided to open his ranch up to hunters. He had heard somewhere of my work in the outdoor field, on radio or television. He wanted to know if he could fly to Kansas City and be a guest on my show to tell the people about his hunting operation. This was about the time the ranchers of Texas started leasing their land to hunters. It soon became a popular and profitable venture. I really don't know where it first started or when. I was constantly looking for material to use on both my radio and my television shows, so we arranged for George to be a guest on my shows. He was very much Texan, and really represented a breed of farmers typical of that generation.

At that time, Kansas City, with its stockyards, was one of the focal points to ship, buy and sell cattle. I can remember when my dad and other neighboring ranchers each year would ship their cattle to the Kansas City market. About all I can remember was watching the train loaded with cattle leaving the little town of Healy, Kansas. It was always a great occasion, because Dad usually brought back presents for us. The last trip he made that I remember, he brought me my first baseball glove. It was a long time ago, but I remember how proud I was to get it.

But back to George Light. It was told that on one trip with cattle to Kansas he rode his horse into the lobby of the famous Muehlebach Hotel. It may be just a story, but knowing George, if he didn't, it was just because he didn't think of it. We were delighted with his appearance on both radio and television. I was impressed with the opportunities his ranch offered in quail, deer and wild boar hunting. We also had several tanks, as he called them, loaded with big bass. He invited us down to hunt or fish, or both. We arranged a date and Dusty and I drove down. His place was everything he said it was. I don't remember doing any fishing. We could hardly believe the number of quail and deer that we found. I don't remember seeing any wild boar, but lots of Javelins. We made two movies for our TV show, and got a lot of material for our radio shows. George was a great guy, and became a good friend.

9

SPEAKING TO OUTDOOR people of good things to eat, just mention wild Morel mushrooms and their faces will light up. Where I lived as a youngster in western Kansas, people were wary of wild mushrooms, due to their lack of knowledge about them. However, no one that I knew would eat them, thinking them to be toxic. I don't think I ever heard of the Morels until I moved to the Ozark countryside. In the spring of the year, people would be excited when it came time for the Morels to burst forth. My first sample tasting of fried Morels convinced me that this was one of the special taste treats God created for man. I was a little skeptical the first time I went mushroom hunting. However, I was assured that there was no way you could mistake a Morel. I soon learned that not only were Morels great for your taste buds, but it was exciting to hunt them. I shot several movies of hunting Morels for my TV show. I received telephone calls from viewers who had found huge mushrooms that they called red mushroom, or beefsteak. I even had people call in and ask to show their big beefsteak mushrooms on my show. The years wore on, and I became as excited about hunting mushrooms as anyone. In the spring of the late '50s, it rained like crazy over the White River watershed in northwest Arkansas and south Missouri. The lowlands of Arkansas were flooded out. There were Corps of Engineer project dams on the White River system, Bull Shoals on the main river, and one on one of its tributaries, the Norfork. As they both had been built for flood control, as well as for power, this was maybe their first big test. They held back the waters of the White with Bull Shoals Dam to protect the flooded lowlands of Arkansas. Lake Bull Shoals was backed up some 40 feet of elevation from power pool level to flood stage.

When they built Bull Shoals Lake, they did not clear the timber. In a short time, the waters of the lake killed all the trees to power pool level. From the power pool level to flood stage elevation, it was solid timber. When the water reached flood stage level, they opened the gates of Bull Shoals Dam. It was an awesome sight, but it made for some great trout fishing below the dam. Above the dam, they held the water back covering the timber long enough to kill all the trees. We caught lots of bass, even in the high water.

We were fortunate to have fished Bull Shoals Lake during the glory years. We fished while it was filling, we fished it at flood stage and elevations in between. At that time, it was rated as one of the top bass lakes in the nation. The year after the flood, after the water receded from the power pool upward, in the spring, the hills were suddenly covered with wild Morels, and the big red ones. It was an unbelievable story. Never had anyone seen anything like it. Even above the water line there were great numbers of Morels under nearly every cedar tree. Fishermen would hire guides to take them out just to hunt mushrooms. I was reminded of the time God was telling Moses about the plagues he was going to send. He told him that things were going to take place that had never happened on the face of the earth, and would never happen again. That's what happened on the Bull Shoals, and will not likely happen again.

About that time the Midwest Ford Dealers advertising committee wanted to hold their annual business meeting and combine it with a fishing trip. I made arrangements for them at Theodosia, Missouri, on the upper end of Bull Shoals. I had fished there many times with my friend Tommy Wilhoit. The dealers were not to meet until Friday and Saturday of that week, so I drove down a couple of days early to fish with Tommy and shoot a bass fishing movie for my TV show. The weather cooperated, although Saturday it rained some. Tommy and I caught lots of bass and had our movie made before the Ford dealers arrived. They caught lots of fish and were happy with their meeting.

Sunday morning, I got myself packed and started home. I usually would go back on Highway 160 to Gainesville, then north on Highway 5 toward Springfield. For some strange reason, I decided to take 160 west toward Branson. I guess you would call it "Wings of Chance." Highway 160 was a narrow, crooked blacktop road. At that time, there were many cedar trees along the roadway, some of them real close to the road, with no fences. I was taking my good easy time, when I noticed Morels underneath almost every cedar tree. I found a place where I could pull off the highway to park my station wagon. I found a brown paper bag in the car, and without closing the door I excitedly started picking Morels. It was absolutely unbelievable! Many cedars had 10 to 15 nice clean mushrooms. I had never seen anything like it. I just kept going from tree to tree and soon had a bag full of mushrooms, but was some 100 yards from my station wagon. Some of the Ford dealers came along and saw my wagon with the door open. They stopped to see if I was in trouble. They thought maybe someone had tried to rob me. They couldn't believe the big sack of Morels, but were happy to share in the find. I can close my eyes 40 years later and see those beautiful Morels. I drove on home, did my TV show live, and taped my radio shows. I called Tommy Wilhoit and told him that I wanted to come back to make a movie, crappie fishing and picking mushrooms. I told him that I would like to bring my wife, Bonnie, and with him and his wife shoot the picture. So we made arrangements and drove down. I asked him if we could have a shore lunch with fried crappie and Morels. We all caught fish and found lots of Morels. We also found several of the red beefsteak mushrooms. We had our shore lunch and filmed it. Bonnie and I drove back to Kansas City.

Monday night I did my live TV show with the movie of shore lunch, with fish and two kinds of wild mushrooms. As I was taking my phone calls at the switchboard, I received a long distance call from Manhattan, Kansas. It was Charles Kramer, a biology professor from Kansas State University. He told me that the so-called beefsteak mushrooms that I had shown on my show could be toxic to some people. He said that you might eat them for years with no consequence, and then boom, it could hit you. I thanked him and told him I would alert my viewers on the next week's show. I did, and I have not eaten any of the red ones since. There are a lot of good edible mushrooms out there, but you need to know what you are doing when you pick them. However, there is no way you can make a mistake on the Morel, so hunt them, pick them, eat them, and enjoy a real taste treat.

Some 40 years have passed. My wife, Bonnie, had lost her bout with cancer, and I was home by myself one evening when the doorbell rang. It was my next-door neighbor, Teresa. She said, "Mr. Ensley, I have a letter for you." My sister was in biology class at Kansas State University in Manhattan. The professor, Charles Kramer, was talking about wild mushrooms. He told them about calling the TV station in Kansas City. He had been watching Harold Ensley on his fishing show cooking wild mushrooms, both the so-called red beefsteak and the Morels. He told the class that he had informed me that the red mushrooms were toxic to some people. He then asked if any of them had watched Harold Ensley, The Sportsman's Friend, on TV. Several hands went up. Teresa's sister said, "My sister in Kansas City lives next door to Ensley." He then asked her to take a letter to her sister to give to me. Teresa handed me the letter. Kramer wanted to know if I remembered his call. He was still teaching biology. However, he had become involved in another venture, dog agility contests. The thing had originated in England and had become popular there. I've always loved dogs, both hunting dogs and pets. He told me the general idea. It sounded like covering and promoting it would make good material for my TV show. I told him that I would like to see his dog perform and possibly film it.

I called a school teacher friend of mine, Dwain Paugh, and asked him to help me. We arranged a date and traveled to Manhattan to meet Professor Charles Kramer and his dog. His dog was a Portuguese water dog. A breed new to me, the dog herself made an amazing story. They were great swimmers, and the Portuguese commercial fishermen used them to haze the schools of fish into their nets. They also used them to send messages from one boat to another. If my information was correct, they could swim as deep as 30 feet. I'm not qualified to go into a discourse about the dogs. Charles set up an official agility course and put his dog through its paces. We filmed the process for my TV show. I also had

Professor Charles Kramer of Kansas State University and his Portuguese water dog Keelee.

87

Charles and his dog Keelee with me when we produced the show. It may have been the first time such an event had been shown on TV here. Now it is a common thing to see dog agility classes on cable TV, and maybe sometimes on the network. I called Charles to ask permission to use a picture of him and his dog in my book. This he seemed pleased to do. He also told me of a new kind of obedience program called Rally-O. He has written a book on it. He told me that this new program was being adopted by the American Kennel Club and will become a title event by January 1, 2003. You can expect to be hearing much more about Rally-O — a rally style of obedience. This all because of a shore lunch of wild mushrooms and fish on my TV show 40-some years ago, and by having a next-door neighbor with a sister at Kansas State University.

"Wings of Chance."

I might also add that Professor Kramer has now retired after teaching 40 years at Kansas State University.

10

A FEW YEARS later, two Ford dealers in Kansas City asked me to take them on an elk hunt in Colorado: Bob Schneider of Schneider Ford and Bennie Benthrop of Broadway Motors. There were 250 Ford dealers in the Kansas City District that sponsored my TV show for 25 years. We had a special working relationship with them. It was almost like family. From the beginning of our relationship, we had a gentleman's agreement that we could fish and hunt with the dealers, but could not use them on our TV show. Many of them loved to hunt and fish. I wish that I could mention each one by name, but that alone would fill a book. We had been with Bennie and Bob on a couple of hunts. Both of them belonged to the Saddle and Sirloin Club of Kansas City. Bob loved to ride horses and thought a pack trip into the mountains of Colorado would be a great experience. I don't think Bennie liked horses that much, but he agreed to go along. I told them that it was getting late to draw for an elk license to hunt in Colorado, but that I would see if there were any elk tags available. I called the director of the Colorado Fish and Game Commission. I told him who I was and that I wanted to know if there were any elk tags yet available for this season. He checked and found that they had several cow elk tags for the area between Creede, Colorado and Pagosa Springs. He said that they had raised the price to $75 per tag.

I told him that we would take four, and asked him if he knew an outfitter in that area. He told me of a man who operated a guest ranch near Bayfield, Colorado, which was just west of Pagosa Springs. He said that his name was Mickey Craig, and gave me his phone number. I called Mickey. I told him my name and what I needed for the elk hunt. We made the necessary arrangements, and I asked him about fishing in the area. I told him of my TV show and wondered if we could come out a couple of weeks before elk season opened and film a TV show. We could shoot movies of a pack trip into the area, do some fishing, and maybe get some pictures of the elk herd before they come down from high country. He told me that his place was on the Pine River, and that there were several high country lakes with lots of trout. We arranged a date. I called a friend of mine, Bill Lott, to go with me.

We left Kansas City right after my TV show and drove all night. The weather was nice, and when we reached the high country, it was a beautiful sight. The Aspen had just turned to gold. I have never seen the Rockies so spectacular! The sight would almost take your breath away. I would take pictures of beautiful scenery, only to drive on and find it more beautiful. We arrived at Mickey's guest ranch about 1 p.m. He had the horses saddled and ready. He said that he had sent his camp chef on ahead to set up camp and have dinner ready for us. My friend Bill was a little older than I, and I didn't know how strong he was. I asked Mickey to take some oxygen along, in case Bill needed it. At that time, I was jogging five or six miles a day. I thought I was in good physical condition for the trip. It was my first trip up into the San Juan wilderness area. The trail led us along the Pine river. I could hardly wait for a chance to fish for trout. Again, it was a trail ride through spectacular scenery. At one time we stopped to rest the horses and we could look across a deep canyon to a waterfall cascading over a cliff. The blue sky, the gold of the Aspen and the waterfalls, God didn't make it any better than that! Mickey turned to me and said, "Ensley, feast your eyes on that!" I will never forget the moment. I can close my eyes and see it now, 35 years later.

We arrived at camp at dusk. The cook had the tents up and a fire going. He soon had a big steak ready and some fried potatoes, and I think he brought a pie with him. The camp was at about 10,000 feet. It was to be our base. From there, we would pack into the high country lakes, shoot a fishing moving, and maybe get some shots of elk. It had been a long day. We had a big feed and retired to our tents. Bill and I were in one tent, and Mickey and his chef were in the other. Tucked into my sleeping bag, I thought to myself how wonderful that God made country like this and has given me the opportunity to see it.

About 3 a.m. I awakened and could hardly breathe. I yelled at Bill to get Mickey and bring the oxygen! I had a terrible pain in my chest and immediately thought of a heart attack. Mickey brought the oxygen. I had never taken oxygen before, but it felt so good. The intense pain was still there, but at least I could breathe. We were a six-hour ride to a telephone, and farther than that from a doctor. I can still see Mickey in his long-handle underwear, standing there in the light of a flashlight. I finally went off to sleep, as did the others. At daybreak, I awakened and everyone was still asleep. I felt of myself to see if I was still alive. I still had the intense pain in my chest. I had kept the others up all night and didn't want to awaken them. I dressed and stepped outside the tent. There had been a heavy frost that night. I was going to saddle my horse and get ready to go back down the mountain when I saw my rod case.

I thought, well, if I'm going to die, I'm going to die fishing! There were two beaver ponds about a hundred yards from the camp. I rigged up my ultra-light spinning outfit, tied on a 1/16-ounce brown Tiny Tot crappie jig, and walked down to the nearest beaver pond. It possibly covered an acre of water. I caught a couple of small trout and released them. Then I saw a big cutthroat. I cast to it and it just inhaled that jig. I was using 2-lb. test line and, having no net, I finally beached it. It was a beautiful cutthroat, possibly 20 inches long. I went back to the tent and awakened everyone.

Mickey said, "Where did you catch that trout?" I told him that I caught it in the beaver pond and that I had seen another one the same size. I was going back and catch it, and I did! It was almost identical to the first one. I asked Bill if he would take my movie camera and get a picture of me with my two cutthroats. He did. Mickey said, "Man, if you can catch trout like that here, wait till you get to the high country lakes."

I said, "Mick, I'm not going any higher. As soon as we can get ready, I must go for a doctor." The cook built a fire, the sun came out, and as it warmed up, I began to feel better. Mick said that we would just fish the Pine River and not go up above the timberline. I decided to try one more day. We fished a beautiful stretch of the Pine. Mick was to catch the trout fly-fishing. I followed him for some two hours. He caught nothing. In desperation, I put my camera down and tied on a cinnamon-colored 1/16-oz. Tiny tot. It just took trout after trout!

Mickey put his fly rod down and borrowed my ultra-light spinning rod. In short order, he caught his limit of trout, as did Bill. The chef didn't go with us. I felt better, but still had that deep pain in my chest. That night the chef fixed a big dinner. You may wonder why I refer to him as the chef and not the camp cook. He was the chef of the guest ranch, and a good one he was! I'm sorry that I cannot recall his name. I decided maybe the big steak and greasy potatoes the night before may have been part of my problem. Therefore, I ate some canned peaches and condensed milk. After a round of conversation about our day's success and some plans for the next day, we crawled into our sleeping bags for the night. All was well for a few hours, until the pain hit me again and I called for the oxygen. So again I had everyone awake at 3:00 in the morning. Then and there I made up my mind that as soon as it became daylight, I was going to saddle my horse and head for home. I finally went to sleep. I awakened before the others, dressed and started making preparations to go down the mountain. I noticed some live coals in the campfire, stirred it around and put on some more wood.

After a good breakfast and breathing in the warm air, I let Mickey persuade me to try one more day. He said, "You're going to love the scenery and the great fishing in Elk Lake." It was some three-hour ride, and at a much higher altitude. He said, "We just might get to see the elk herd for your pictures." This day the chef decided to go with us. He said that he was not that much of a fisherman, but it would be better than just staying around camp. It was a beautiful ride and the scenery was spectacular. We didn't see the elk, but had some fantastic trout fishing. Guess who caught the largest trout and the most fish; the chef! I was on camera and loaned him an ultra-light spinning outfit. I got a big kick out of the chef. He didn't know what he was doing, but he caught fish. It was the case of the novice catching fish more often than the expert. You have probably seen it happen! "Wings of Chance."

The next day, Mick took Bill and me to Little Flint Lake. I guess it was a glacier lake above the timberline. The ride to the lake was over the roughest, steepest mountain trail you could imagine. I dismounted to take pictures, and finally just climbed the rest of the way to the lake. Bill was so nervous from the ride that he didn't feel like fishing when we reached a boulder-strewn flat at the edge of the lake. He stayed with the horses. The lake was a rather small, circular lake surrounded by steep, rocky slopes. Mick led the way as we stumbled over boulders. I was carrying my camera and my ultra-light spinning rod. After about 150 yards across from the horses, Mick stopped to fish. The shoreline was steep, and the depth of the water dropped off sharply. We were using 2-lb. test line and 1/16-oz. crappie jigs. In short order, we caught two nice trout. Mickey was carrying a chain stringer; he put the fish on it and fastened it down with a rock. We beat the water to a froth for about an hour, with nothing, so we decided to walk the perimeter of the lake, fishing as we went.

It probably was a mile around the edge of the lake to the horses. It was a miserable walk over the boulders on the slope of the shoreline. The temperature had dropped sharply, and we hadn't caught one fish. When we reached the horses, we had some sandwiches that the chef had packed for us. Bill had a miserable time! Besides being cold, he was about sick from the thought of riding down that trail. He said, "Harold, do we have to go down that same trail?" I said, "Yes, unless you want to spend the rest of your life up here." Mick said, "We still have a little time, but we just as well go back to camp." I asked him if he wanted to leave those two trout on the stringer where we had tied them earlier. Mick said that he would go get them. It was only about 150 yards, so I told him I would go with him. I took my ultra-light spinning gear, but left my movie camera with Bill and the horses. Mick took the ultra-light outfit that he was using and we stumbled around to the spot. I had tied on a 1/18-oz. white marabou jig, and as Mick was getting the stringer, I made a cast. With a 1/18-oz. jig on 2 lb test line, I got some distance on the cast. I thought I'd just let that jig go down till it hit bottom. If I get hung up, I'll just break it off and we'll leave. I was watching the line as the jig sank slowly. When the line reached a 70-degree angle, I saw the line twitch. I set the hook and had a nice trout. I yelled for Bill to bring the camera. He did and took a picture of me with the fish. We proceeded to catch a limit of nice trout and finish the movie. And all because we went back to get two fish on a stringer.

"Wings of Chance."

It was getting late and we still had to ride down that treacherous trail. We made part of it before darkness set in. Bill was almost beside himself. When a grown man keeps saying, "Whoa, boy," to the female horse he's riding, he has to be pretty nervous! The last mile of the trail we covered in pure darkness, and just as we reached the edge of the clearing at camp, my horse stumbled and fell. I wasn't hurt, but I promised myself never again to ride in high country after dark. The chef had a big fire going and a big dinner. I hurt that night, but didn't need oxygen.

I had planned the next day to go back to the ranch, but Mick had other plans. He said, "For three days you had so many trout on your crappie jigs; today you and I are going to wade Flint Creek. I want to see what you can do!"

That morning the chef and Bill broke camp, left us some sandwiches, and saddled the horses. They took the pack animals with them. Mick and I put on our waders and started wading and fishing up flint Creek. Only in Alaska have I seen trout fishing like we had that day. Time just got away from us! Late in the afternoon, I told Mick we should be going. It was a six-hour ride down a rugged mountain trail to his ranch. We fished on a ways and headed back to our campsite.

It was almost dark when we saddled our horses and started down the trail. I couldn't believe that I got myself into that kind of situation, riding a horse down a rugged mountain trail for six hours on a dark night. It was midnight when we reached the ranch. By that time, my chest was really hurting, and I thought, we did all this to prepare for an elk hunt. The next day Bill and I drove back to Kansas City in time to get my movie film processed and edited for my show. I had been to see my doctor. He told me that I had virus pneumonia and a severe attack of pleurisy, and was going to put me in the hospital. I told him that I had never missed a TV show in 15 years. I asked him if it would be too dangerous for me to do my TV show and then go to the hospital. He told me it would be okay, but to call him immediately if something happened.

My wife said, "Doc, tell him to quit jogging!" He said, "Bonnie, if he hadn't been a jogger, he probably would have died on the mountain." I kept my string going and went on to complete 25 years of doing a weekly 30-minute show, live, without missing one. I promised myself again I would never ride a horse over a mountain trail at night. But wait until you read the elk-hunting trip that came as a result of that pack trip.

I had pretty well recovered from chest problems when we had to leave for the elk hunt. The four of us, Bennie Benthroup, Bob Schneider, and Dusty and I, drove to Colorado. We spent the first night in a small town near Creede, Colorado. We were supposed to meet Mickey at a campsite just below the Rio Grande Reservoir. We arrived at the camp area about 10:30 a.m. Mickey was to meet us at 11 a.m. with the horses and pack animals. Mickey had set up two hunting camps in the high country. He had 23 hunters from various parts of the country coming in to hunt. All parties had arrived at the 11 a.m. time, and no Mickey! Twelve o'clock came and no Mickey! Then one o'clock and no Mickey!

When Mickey didn't show by 4 p.m., two hunters from Illinois said to Dusty and me, "We have some cooking oil and some utensils in our camper, Ensley. Why don't you catch us some trout and we'll have something to eat?" Dusty and I had a couple of ultra-light spinning rods in my station wagon. We walked the short distance to the stream below the dam. Using 1/16-oz. crappie jigs, in short order we had twelve trout. It was almost dusk when we started cleaning fish, and Mickey and his guides showed up. It so happened that bears had gotten into both base camps, tore up the tents and scattered the horses. I just assumed that we would all go into Creede and stay at a motel. Not so! Mick told us to get our guns and gear, that we were going over the mountain to the camps. By this time, darkness had set in and the temperature started falling. I was holding one of the pack animals. The animals' packs were already loaded, and we were waiting to get the entire group ready. I had been holding the animal for about 30 minutes when one of the hunters from Oklahoma City came along. I asked him to hold the horse while I stretched my legs a bit. He gladly took the halter rope, and I went on my way. About 30 minutes later I walked back. It was almost dark.

As I came up, he didn't recognize me and said, "Have you seen Harold?" I asked him what he wanted with him. He said, "I'm getting tired of holding this horse." It became a by-word around camp and everyone got a kick out of it. They finally got everyone's gear packed and we were ready to start up the mountain trail. You can imagine what it took for a party of 23 hunters. It was now 9 p.m., and I thought to myself that I had promised that I would never ride a horse over a rough mountain trail at night, and here I was, about to start a five-hour ride to the camp. I was leading a pack animal because the hunter ahead of me had been drinking. He could hardly stay on his horse. He dropped the reins and was holding the saddle horn to steady himself. In the dim light, I could see him swaying from side to side. I kept telling him to hang on. I don't know how he made it, but he did! My pack animal kept pulling back and finally pulled the rope from my hands. I was cold, and no way was I going to dismount on that narrow trail, in the middle of a pack train, to pick up the rope. The animal could neither go backwards nor get off the trail, so I thought I would just let him follow. Somewhere along the trail, we split, with one group going to one camp, and the rest of us to the other. We arrived at our camp about 3 a.m. We were cold and hungry. The cook had some hot stew for us. By 4 a.m. we went to our tents. Bob, Bennie, Dusty and I were in one tent. The cook had put a bucket of water in our tent and already there was about half an inch of ice on it. I just crawled into my sleeping bag with my clothes on and was comfortable.

The next day the four of us had two elk. It was a beautiful day, but cold. I shall never forget the sound of a bull elk as it cut loose of a bugle just before sunrise. The air was calm and crisp, and the elk was just below us in a canyon. What a thrill! The last day, as we prepared to go back down the mountain, Mickey asked me to go with him to get some pictures of a trophy bull elk that one of the party had shot. He said, "It's only a three-hour ride, and we can ride from there back down the mountain to meet the others at the car, and that Dusty could take Bennie and Bob down the trail and meet us."

I should have known better, but agreed to do it. Mick saddled the horses, packed the two cow elk on pack animals, and we followed the hunter to shoot pictures of his trophy elk. It was cold, but the sun was shining. You would never believe the steep, rugged trail our horses climbed to get to the other side of the mountain. It was scary, but beautiful. I shot movies as we went along, but in no way did it show how treacherous it was. When we reached the summit, you could see for miles, a spectacular view. We reached the man's elk about 3 p.m. and shot the pictures we needed.

Mick wanted to go down into another canyon for another elk. I said, "Mick, it's getting late and we need to be heading to the car." He finally consented and said that we would have to find a game trail down the other side. He told me that he had never been that way. We didn't have much choice; it was a five-hour ride back to the hunting camp, then another five-hour ride to the car at the base of the Rio Grande dam.

As Mickey led the two pack animals across the summit, I had what I thought was a brilliant idea. I told Mickey I wanted to ride back a ways and get a picture of him riding over the ridge until he disappeared from view, then to come back to get me. We got the shots and he was gone awhile. When he came back, he told me that he didn't see a trail down the other side, except for a narrow path across a rockslide. He thought if we could cross it, we might find our way down the mountain. He said that he would ride across leading the pack animals and, if he made it, I could follow, and if he didn't make it, for me to ride back to camp for help. The mountainside was a rockslide at about a 45-degree angle. The path was so narrow that the horses had to put one foot in front of the other. He worked his way slowly and carefully across. The rockslide was probably 100 feet across. He made it safely, stopped the horses and yelled, "Hey, Champ, you try it!" He always called me Champ. My horse made it safely.

Mickey said, "If we can reach the mesa below, we will be above a small lake and from there down there is a ranger trail that I know."

We circled the edge of the mesa. Mick yelled back and told me he could find no trail down to the lake. If we couldn't, we were in deep trouble, for there was no way back. I told Mick that I had noticed a spot in some underbrush where it appeared to have been used by elk. We backtracked until we found it. Mick said, "We'll have to try it." He put his horse through the underbrush and almost dropped out of sight. He pulled back on the horse's head until it was almost sliding down on its rear end. He was leading two pack animals. He called for me to follow. We made it down to the lake safely.

To this day I can't believe what we did! It was almost dark when we reached the ranger trail below the lake. It was smoothing sailing for the first hour, but we still had a rough trail ahead of us. Then darkness really set in. I could barely see the pack animals ahead of me. Finally, we came to an abrupt halt. Mick called back and said that he was lost. We had to turn the horses around on a very narrow trail. About an hour later, we reached a point where we could see the lights of my station wagon on the campground below. Dusty, Bennie and Bob were about to give up on us and drive into Creede. Not many times in my lifetime have I been through or seen anything like that! I was so happy to have made it back safely that I felt like Bennie, who had said, "I just made two trips, my first and my last!"

When we arrived back safely at Kansas City, Bennie would tell his friends about the trip. Every time he told it, the temperature dropped a few degrees, the altitude a thousand feet higher, and the trail was steeper and rougher. I had promised myself after the first trip that I would never ride a horse in Colorado country again. It had happened again, but for certain that was the last time! I made many more trips back into Colorado's high country to fish, but never to ride a horse over a dangerous mountain trail in the dark. All elk hunting trips are not that way. My hunting and fishing buddy, Jim Higgins, brought me some elk steaks. They were so good I was almost ready to go back to high country.

11

ONE OF THE amazing stores of the present time is the explosion of the deer and wild turkey population in our country. This, of course, has brought about the numbers of deer and wild turkey hunters. It includes both genders. Growing numbers of women have become dedicated to hunting either wild turkey or deer or both! My late wife, Bonnie, was a dedicated quail hunter. Because of her intense desire to learn and her dedication, to my surprise she became an excellent quail hunter. She would hunt ducks and geese, but her real love was taking the dogs and hunting quail. She had no desire to shoot a deer or wild turkey.

My friend Martin Hamann of Mason, Wisconsin is an avid deer hunter and a good one. He sent me this picture of his 12-year-old daughter with her first buck. He also sent me some interesting statistics about deer hunting in that state. In the year 2000 there were 694,111 hunters for the gun season, and 7% of them were women. Zoe Caywood, who operates War Eagle Mill in War Eagle, Arkansas, is a prime example. She has shot her share of wild turkey. At the moment, she is the only person, man or woman, who has shot all five species of wild turkey with a muzzle-loader! It's little wonder about Zoe, for her dad, Jewell Medlin, was a dedicated big game hunter. He didn't fish all that much. However, we must tell you about a fish he caught with us.

First, I want to give you just a few more short statistics. This is to show you how deer and wild turkey hunting has expanded here in the Midwest. In Missouri, in the year 1944, 589 deer were taken. In 1947, 5519 were taken. In 2002, in Missouri, 250,910 deer were taken. In Missouri, in 1959, a turkey permit was $5, and an estimated 3,000 hunters had taken 60 birds. In the year 2001, 55,302 birds were taken. It's almost unbelievable. Another interesting statistic: in Missouri, way back in 1959, an estimated six million rabbits were harvested. The same growth in the number of both men and women taking to the fields has taken place in many other states. What's amazing is the growth in the numbers of bow hunters. Recently, some 90,000 bow hunters were reported to have harvested over 15,000 deer during the season.

Recently, I asked a friend of mine, Gene Fox, who works for the Missouri Conservation Commission, if he would like to hunt deer with the type of bows and arrows used by the Indians. Gene is an avid hunter, both with guns and with a bow. He laughed and told me that he didn't think he would even try. Certainly, improvements to the modern types of bows and arrows have played a prominent part in the growth of archery hunting.

However, getting back to Zoe Caywood and her turkey-hunting prowess. Her dad, Jewell, was the Ford dealer for many years in Lamar, Missouri. As we said before, he didn't fish all that much but was a dedicated big game hunter. One time, C.A. White, the

12-year-old Ashley Hamann of Mason, Wisconsin, with her first buck.

Ford dealer in Nevada, Missouri, persuaded Jewell to go with him, Dusty and me to Baudette, Minnesota for some walleye fishing. We could not use either of them on that TV show, but they just wanted to fish with us. The first day, Jewell didn't even go out with us. We shot a lot of movies for my TV show but, of course, didn't use anything with C.A. in it. The next day we persuaded Jewell to go with us. He had an old spin-casting reel on a broken glass rod. He had overlapped the two pieces of rods and taped them together. I tied on a 3/8-oz. marabou jig. He made a cast and let the lure sink to the bottom of the lake. He picked up the line and started to reel in. The rod bent double. He said, "I'm hung up in the rocks!" I saw the rod tip quiver, and told him he had a fish on. We coached him the best we could, and he landed the fish, a 13-1/2-lb. walleye. It was unbelievable, and I couldn't use it for my TV show because he was a Ford dealer. Here was a guy who had never fished for walleye, and the first cast out, with a broken casting rod, he catches the largest walleye taken that year in that part of Minnesota. He won all kinds of prizes for the biggest walleye caught in the Baudette area.

"Wings of Chance."

I have fished some 50 years for walleye and 11-1/4 lbs. is the largest I've taken anywhere. Some 20 years ago, when I was giving a fish filleting demonstration in the Wal-Mart store in Lamar, Missouri, Jewell brought the mounted walleye into the store to remind me of the story. He was a great friend and a great hunter. His daughter, Zoe, is carrying on the tradition. Men, you might just as well move over, the ladies are coming on!

Zoe Caywood of War Eagle, Arkansas, with her wild turkey in Yucatan, Mexico.

SPECIAL MOMENTS TO REMEMBER

Start of 50 years of broadcasting outdoor programs.

A special day, fishing with Joe DiMaggio.

Teaching my friend, Helen Walton, to fish near Bella Vista, Arkansas, with our guide, Wes Sands.

Shore lunch with "Doc" of Gunsmoke and his pilot in Canada.

My only hunting picture with my son, Smokey, after goose hunting in Colorado.

The Wendt boys, David and Dan, with the 100-lb. watermelon they brought to my show, raised by their father, Otto Wendt, in the Kaw Valley near Kansas City. Forty years later, one of the boys bought my book at a Wal-Mart store.

Trophy guapote, the most illusive fish of the Rain Forest jungle of Costa Rica, with my wife Bonnie and Herman, our guide.

My wife Bonnie and me, with trophy golden trout from the Bridger Wildlife Area of Wyoming. This is still one of the highlights of my life.

Country Squire helping me do a commercial for Strongheart Dog Food.

My trademark for my television years, a red Ford country sedan. Most of my generation remember me for the car, my bird dog Country Squire and my theme song, "Gone Fishin'."

Jogging with Charlie Plum to raise money for Cystic Fibrosis. Jogging was also a big part of my life, during and in between fishing and hunting.

Fishing and hunting were special in my life, but I also loved gardening! Gardening proof that you can grow sweet potatoes that look like ducks.

God's great miracles can be seen in your garden every day. You sow a tiny seed and it comes forth into a plant and bears fruit. It's amazing!

Picking cucumbers from a ladder.

Tying up my tomato vines from a ladder.

I do raise tomatoes (and cucumbers)!

My daughter, Sandy, with her first tarpon in Costa Rica.

"Breakfast of Champions" with Buck O'Neil and Norm Stewart.

Two of my favorite fishing buddies, the late Darryl Porter and Pete LaCock.

A much appreciated tribute to me from my home town of Healy, Kansas.

We had just completed writing our second book, "Wings of Chance," and putting the pictures together, when I received this picture from Wisconsin of Ashley Hamann. She is the 16-year-old daughter of my special friends, Martin and his wife. Ashley had just shot her first buck with a bow. As a special tribute to Ashley and all the teenage boys and girls who love to hunt, fish and love God's outdoor world, we present this picture of Ashley and her first buck. Our sincere congratulations to Ashley Hamann of Ashland, Wisconsin.

FRESH-WATER PRESIDENT

Sirs:

Re Kansas City's World Champion Fresh-water Fisherman Harold Ensley (FACES IN THE CROWD, Nov. 14). I know a lot of people look like Harry Truman —but this is ridiculous! (*See below.*)

JOHN A. RIDDLE

Pittsburgh, Pa.

HAROLD

HARRY

Good Luck — & be sure you have a guard!

2/7/61 *Harry Truman*

A tribute to a special hunting buddy of many years — Mr. Sam Walton.